Praise for *The Inner Game of Selling*

"I believe selling is the same everywhere, and Ron has testified to that in this land of Japan. By using the principles found in this book, our people's sales increased, on average, more than 26 percent."

—Minoru Asai, Managing Director, ERA Japan Corporation

"*The Inner Game of Selling* takes a much needed look inside the mind of the sales performer, where we can either create abundance or fabricate roadblocks. This book shows how we can align our feelings, attitudes, and behaviors with our goals to deploy our true talents. A must-read for anyone who wants to win in selling and in life."

—Gerhard Gschwandtner, founder and Publisher, Selling Power

"The most comprehensive and practical book I've seen on goal development and overcoming barriers to achievement."

—Simon Walter, Director, Beca Infrastructure Ltd., Auckland, New Zealand

"The dean of relationship-based selling has taken his game to the next level with *The Inner Game of Selling*. Willingham has synthesized modern human behavioral science with the very best concepts associated with emotional intelligence and delivered an interactive self-coaching masterpiece. Whether you are in the business of selling, leading, or participating as a member of the human race, this book is the bedrock to living a more fulfilling and productive life."

—Jeff Hughes, CEO GAMA International

"I can't wait to share *The Inner Game of Selling* and observe the results that will follow."

—Michael Fann, Chief Operating Officer, Just Water International Limited, Auckland, New Zealand

The Inner Game of Selling

Free Press

Mastering

the

Hidden Forces

That Determine

Your

Success

Ron Willingham

NEW YORK   LONDON   TORONTO   SYDNEY

FREE PRESS
A Division of Simon & Schuster, Inc.
1230 Avenue of the Americas
New York, NY 10020

FREE PRESS and colophon are trademarks of Simon & Schuster, Inc.

For information about special discounts for bulk purchases,
please contact Simon & Schuster Special Sales:
1-800-456-6798 or business@simonandschuster.com

DESIGNED BY PAUL DIPPOLITO

Manufactured in the United States of America

10 9 8 7 6 5 4 3 2 1

Library of Congress Cataloging-in-Publication Data

Willingham, Ron, 1932–
    The inner game of selling : mastering the hidden forces that
determine your success / Ron Willingham.
        p.   cm.
    Includes index.
    1. Selling. I. Title.
    HF5438.25.W533 2006
    658.85—dc22
    2006041042
ISBN-13: 978-0-7432-8628-2
ISBN-10:   0-7432-8628-6

To my special friend Joe Barnett . . .

Because you came into my life with your positive encouragement and friendship, I found myself in this incredible business of helping people discover their better selves.

In a person's whole lifetime there may be two or three special people who help us make choices that then lead to significant life directions.

You were one of them, my friend.

There's no way that I can ever repay you.

Special Thanks

To Sarah Granstrom, Roneal Sweet, and Robin Willingham for your help with word processing, editing, and—most of all—your patience.

To all the salespeople who have participated in our Integrity Selling course around the world: what I have learned from you has been invaluable in digging down to the real reasons why salespeople sell.

To super agents Jane Dystel and Miriam Goderich. As usual you made the business process easy.

To Fred Hills, for the chance to work with a seasoned pro who knows, cares, and understands my message. Your guidance and personal editing have been much appreciated.

And finally, to all my fellow salespeople who endure all the day-to-day challenges and rewards that this wonderful profession offers us.

The New Context of Selling

Your ability to sell is much more an issue of
who you are than *what* you know.

This changes the whole context of
what it takes to be successful in selling.

It's the sum of your inner values and beliefs that
regulates and controls your sales success.

To the extent these are strengthened and expanded,
your sales success will automatically grow.
Until then, it will probably stay the same.

Contents

Introduction: How This Book Can Help You   *1*

1. Self-Understanding
Discovering Why You Sell What You Sell   *13*

2. Boundaries
Examining Your Current Belief Boundaries   *35*

3. Breakthrough
Shattering Blockages of Your Success   *56*

4. Achievement
Understanding the Four Core Success Factors   *76*

5. Abundance
Setting Goals for the Future You   *96*

6. Creativity
Discovering Your Creative Goal-Seeking Mechanism   *117*

7. Customer Focus
How to Sell the Way Customers Want to Buy   *136*

8. Energy
Releasing Unlimited Achievement Drive   *153*

9. Control
Handling the Emotional Side of Selling   *169*

10. Social Skills
Helping People Feel Understood   187

11. Self-Talk
Choosing What to Say When You Talk to Yourself   204

12. Purpose
Finding Meaning in What You Do   221

13. Values
Deciding What You Stand For   237

Afterword   253

New Discoveries About Sales Success

1. You have an inner belief boundary that defines who you are, what's possible for you to sell, and what life rewards you deserve to enjoy.

2. This boundary is based on your past perceptions, and not on actual fact or truth.

3. You live out these inner beliefs without questioning their authenticity.

4. You have a strong inner need to hold on to these old beliefs and experience difficulty releasing them.

5. Your sales and life circumstances won't significantly change until you release the need to hold on to these old beliefs and move past them to new goals.

A man cannot directly *choose his circumstances, but he can choose his thoughts, and so indirectly, yet surely, shape his circumstances.*

—JAMES ALLEN

Introduction

How This Book Can Help You

LET ME JUST SAY IT!

If you don't intellectually know and unconsciously practice what's in this book, you absolutely can't be as successful in your sales career as you should be.

An audacious statement? Maybe.

But all I ask of you is to digest the ideas in this book, carefully following my step-by-step directions, and then decide whether or not my statement is correct.

See if you don't suddenly begin to sell on much higher levels.

How You Sell Isn't As Important As Why You Sell

I suspect that most of your formal sales training or education involves *how to sell.* Maybe you were unlucky enough to have been taught things like closing techniques, negotiation strategies, or other persuasive gimmicks. Maybe you were even more confused by motivators, speakers, or trainers who taught you tricky closes and stuff like how to overcome stalls and objections, tie-downs, nail-downs, or other similar ploys to make weaker people acquiesce to your power and finesse.

Wonderful!

Wouldn't you just love to have stuff like that done to you?

In this book I'll show you how to sell with high integrity, honesty, and impeccable ethics. A way that will allow you to feel good and will honor and value your customers.

But I must be clear: to lift yourself to your highest possible levels of sales success, *why you sell* is infinitely more important than *how you sell*. So most of this book is about that.

In it I'll share with you the real reasons for your expanded success in selling—the deepest causes of high performance that only a few people know. I'll also expose many old destructive selling myths, some of which are still being taught today.

You'll discover for yourself why most so-called "sales skills" are either too shallow or too manipulative to actually work. In many cases they actually prevent you from enjoying the level of success that could otherwise be yours. They become your enemies, leading you down the wrong path.

When you internalize my directions and make them your own, you'll emerge a different salesperson. You'll view yourself and your career possibilities in a whole new, expanded way. You'll develop a stronger *abundance mentality* and *prosperity consciousness*. These are beliefs or viewpoints that manifest themselves in your selling behaviors. You'll identify and cast off old emotional shackles that have kept you from the success you're capable of enjoying.

Above all, you'll release yourself from the need to hang on to old, limiting beliefs.

The Truth Comes Out

Here's the truth: at least 80 percent of all salespeople don't sell well. One reason is that they have a totally erroneous view of what the selling process is. Most go about it wrong. Tragically, many don't even know that they don't know. Add this to the fact that they also have an inadequate view of their actual possibilities, and you can clearly see why they don't succeed.

How can they be successful with a foundation built on these weaknesses?

These misunderstandings confine them to low income levels, and cause poor retention in many sales organizations. Observe most of the people who attempt to sell you things, and you'll probably come away less than impressed with the way you're treated. You don't believe me? Then try to buy a car, or a computer, or a cell phone. Check out the different salespeople, and see how much they really care about you and your needs.

What gives me the right to ask these questions and make such statements?

Good question.

Why I've Earned the Right To Write

I've been earning money by selling since I was eight years old. I've always wanted to be a salesperson. With the exception of two months of my adult life, I've been compensated by how much I sold or how much my sales organization earned.

Over 1.5 million people have graduated from my development courses. Our Integrity Selling course has been taught in eighty nations and has been translated into several languages. All kinds of people—from a wide range of cultures, businesses, and product lines—have found our processes beneficial.

Our firm, Integrity Systems, claims numerous blue-chip clients, such as Johnson & Johnson, The Guardian Life Insurance Company, American Red Cross, IBM, Principal Financial Group, USAA, Morgan Stanley, Abbott Labs, sanofi-aventis, Franklin Templeton, GE Financial Services, Coldwell Banker, and scores of other organizations, large and small.

They choose us because we help them enjoy results in the form of increased sales, salesperson retention, and customer satisfaction. It's not uncommon for a client to experience increases of 15 to 25 percent. A group of Coldwell Banker agents collectively increased their sales 331 percent. Outstanding isn't it?

It Isn't *What* You Know

Your sales success isn't an issue of what you know; rather, it's the result of who you are! Who you are is the sum total of your knowledge, values, ethical standards, self-beliefs, emotional and spiritual strengths, and other things known and unknown.

This is where most so-called books on selling miss the boat. It isn't that they're all wrong; a few have some good ideas. It's just that they don't go deep enough. They don't get close to the real issues that determine your ability to sell to your real potential.

It's true that you must possess a good deal of knowledge—product, industry, technology, other kinds. This only gives you a ticket to get into the arena, it doesn't help you win games. Being highly successful demands something much deeper than mere knowledge.

Unfortunately, your whole educational experience probably caused you to believe that knowledge is power. This is the familiar mantra that the great gurus chant. But this simply isn't true.

Knowledge is only power when we apply it toward a worthy goal. We'll be blocked from doing this when it's not congruent with our *unconscious views* of our possibilities, values, and perceived abilities.

The Inner Game: An Issue of Internal Congruence

The real reason why people sell well involves key emotional and spiritual factors that must be aligned before you're released to perform on higher levels. Until this happens you'll always be emotionally handcuffed, and unconsciously barred from moving out into the deeper waters of success.

Here are some main factors that must come into congruence within you.

The Sales Congruence Model

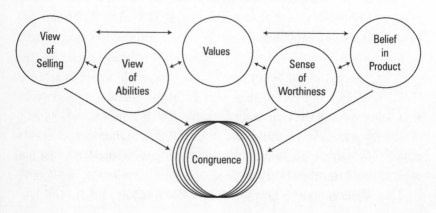

You'll learn that you're a holistic system—body, mind, spirit—composed not only of knowledge, but also of values, internal beliefs, habits, and automatic emotions. You'll understand how these and other forces within you operate in the physical body to produce certain programmed behaviors.

All five of these dimensions must be in congruence for you to sell to your highest potential. If you try to sell a product or service that conflicts with your inner values, or that you don't believe creates value for customers, you'll experience inner conflicts. Likewise, if you don't believe you have the abilities to do it, you'll emotionally handcuff yourself.

Let me quickly define each of these five dimensions. I'll expand on them later on.

View of Selling

View of selling is your internal belief about what the selling process really is. Is it something you do *to* people, or something you do *for* them? Is it persuading and convincing, or identifying and satisfying wants or needs people have?

Interview ten people and ask them what they think of when they hear the words *sales* or *salesman,* and most will respond negatively. What does this tell you?

I define selling as a process of identifying and filling people's wants or needs, and creating value for them. It's a mutual win-win activity, where both sides benefit from the transaction.

View of Abilities

View of abilities is your internal belief about who you are, how capable you are, and what levels of success you *deserve* to enjoy. Each of us has our own internal set of beliefs about what's possible for us to achieve. Our unconscious beliefs are so powerful that they blind us to opportunities, results, and goals that are outside our current mental paradigms.

Simply put, if we don't internally believe that a higher level of sales is possible for us, we'll ignore, or not even recognize, opportunities that would surely accelerate us to these higher sales levels. We'll often unconsciously set out to prove the goal is impossible.

Values

Values are the rules or internal guidelines by which you live your life. They determine the boundaries of your behavior. They define what you will do and what you won't do—what your appropriate life responses are, and what they're not.

Salespeople are often asked to do selling activities that conflict with their values. When people are expected to act in ways that conflict with their values, internal stress is created. But when they perform consistently with their values, they exhibit energy and confidence. Both the salesperson and the customer feel good about the relationship.

Sense of Worthiness

Each of us has, over our lifetime of experiences, developed deep, profound, unconscious beliefs about who we are and what we *deserve* to have in the way of life rewards.

Buried deeply within the caverns of our emotional and spiritual psyches is a well-established set of self-beliefs. Although they're hidden from our conscious knowledge, they reign supreme in guiding all our actions, feelings, behaviors, and abilities. They send silent signals that say to us, "Here's the level of success, rewards, or prosperity you deserve to enjoy." Then, without questioning their rightness or wrongness, we carry them out in our sales behavior. We rarely, if ever, really analyze why we think, believe, and act the way we do.

This sense of worthiness is inextricably tied to our individual self-images, which were molded by our responses to the whole of our life experiences. It permeates our most entrenched emotional and spiritual sense of significance.

More than anything else, this self-perception defines our selling success. We *must* act and perform consistent with it. We *can't* act otherwise, despite all our conscious efforts.

This is why traditional "sales skills" don't work. In fact, when they're inconsistent with our deep self-beliefs, they usually weaken our ability to sell successfully.

Belief in Product

Belief in product is believing that what we're selling gives customers value exceeding the cost. As this belief is internalized, it becomes a conviction that then motivates us to create as much value for customers as we can. When we focus on creating extra value for customers and know that we'll be rewarded consistently, we tap into vast new reservoirs of confidence and energy.

This then motivates us to higher and higher sales success. A sense of integrity, or authenticity, is subliminally communicated to customers. Trust develops. We sell more. Customers are happier and more loyal.

There's always a silent, powerful force at work when we believe that the value we create outweighs the prices we charge. This attitude is communicated spontaneously, even unconsciously. It gives us confidence and power, and creates a sense of trust to our customers.

Understanding the Model

Look again at the Sales Congruence Model and consider the following points:

1. Conflicts or low sales levels result wherever gaps occur between the dimensions.
2. The wider the gap, the more salespeople suffer internal stress.
3. Conflicts or stress cause mental and emotional blocks that inhibit sales success.
4. As conflicts are reduced, sales, personal confidence, and communication increase.
5. Bringing dimensions into congruence is an emotional issue, not an intellectual learning process.
6. The dimensions only come together when positive actions, attitudes, and values are practiced in your everyday selling activities.

The Inner Game of Selling is about bringing these dimensions into harmony or congruence. I can't stress enough that this is not an intellectual process, but rather an emotional one.

As you reflect on what I've presented, you'll quickly see that I'm challenging you to think differently about yourself and the whole selling process.

But thinking differently isn't always easy to do, unless you have a strong desire to perform differently. Your thinking predicts your future performance.

Not How to Sell, but How to Think Differently

My purpose is to help you sell like the pro you were destined to become. But I can't achieve this by just teaching you sales skills. To accomplish my goal, I must help you *think* differently. You must view selling and your abilities in new ways and come to understand your actual possibilities.

Since your behaviors are driven by your inner values, thoughts, and beliefs, and not by your conscious discipline, we'll go to the source. You'll first change your *thinking,* which will change your *inner beliefs,* and then your *behaviors* will automatically change. It's cause and effect.

But let me be more specific about how this book can help you.

How This Book Can Help You

Throughout this book, I'll present concepts, and then more important, I'll lay out proven successful Action Guides for you to practice. As you faithfully apply these, you'll enjoy a Discovery Learning process that only comes from experience. You'll enjoy the following results as you practice the success principles I'll outline. All these will lead you to higher sales success and/or earnings.

1. You'll learn how to sell people the way they want to buy.
2. You'll develop stronger levels of self-confidence.
3. You'll experience more positive responses and respect from people.
4. You'll quickly separate yourself from ordinary salespeople.
5. You'll immediately cause customers to notice your uniqueness, trust you, and want to do business with you.
6. You'll develop a dynamic prosperity consciousness that will know no limits.

7. You'll be referable—your customers will want to help you expand your business.
8. Your view of your actual possibilities will continually expand.
9. Your thirst to grow and develop will lead you into ever-increasing levels of knowledge and wisdom.
10. Your intellectual, emotional, and spiritual dimensions will be stimulated, begging for greater discernment.

Just think what your life can be like when you experience these benefits.

A Book to be Practiced, Not Just Read

This is a self-help action book. Just read it and you'll gain new knowledge, but your sales probably won't improve substantially. For you to enjoy increases you must take action and practice the Action Guides and exercises I lay out for you.

I have included specific activities that have helped real salespeople increase their sales and personal growth. You may or may not do all of the ones I suggest. That's okay, because you can come back later and apply different ones at different times in the future.

The book is designed to be an ongoing learning and success guide. As you practice these ideas I share with you, you'll quickly discover that you can continue to learn them on many levels.

You will discover a number of key concepts that will be emphasized again and again throughout the book. This repetition is intentional. It is almost like a mantra that we repeat to ourselves until it is ingrained into our unconscious and becomes part of our belief system. We then act on them as matter of habit. Then you will have the confidence to move to new levels of success that you never before thought possible.

How to Gain the Most from This Book

To achieve maximum benefits from each chapter, please follow these suggestions:

1. Scan the entire book first to get an idea of its content.
2. Come back and spend a few days or a week reading and reviewing

one of the chapters. Digest the thoughts, and apply them in your daily selling activities.

3. Underline key points, make notes on the pages, and write Action Guides or other ideas on index cards and carry them as reminders.

4. Then spend a few days on each chapter practicing this same active process.

As you take action and apply the suggestions I give you, you'll transform the concepts into automatic behaviors. Only by application will you enjoy steady increases in your self-beliefs, prosperity consciousness, and sales.

An Assumption

I am of course assuming that you're eager to learn. One trait I've noticed in highly successful people is that the more you learn, the more you learn there is to learn.

I've met very few high achievers who are satisfied with where they are. Their hunger, their drive, the motivation that got them to where they are usually intensifies as they become more successful.

I've never gotten close to mastering, to perfection, the success principles I write about.

As you begin this journey with a hunger to learn more, become more, and serve your customers more, you'll have an exciting and productive adventure.

My Hope for You

My hope is that this book will guide you to expand your own *area-of-the-possible* and move into the free-flowing, rarified atmosphere of abundance that beckons your embrace. That it will reveal to you vast new vistas of potential that you've been unable to see before.

Please suspend judgment as to whether my promises are valid, and just say, "Well, maybe he's got something that will help me! I'll give it a try!"

Expect some breakthroughs. No matter where you are today, remind yourself daily, "Why limit myself? Why not open my life up to greater prosperity and abundance?"

Think in terms of new, expanded life possibilities: how you'll feel when you reach larger and larger goals, earn greater respect and trust from customers, enjoy increased sales and personal rewards, and develop an expanded abundance mentality.

In summary, to rise above your previous levels of success you must learn to think differently. Only then will you begin to act differently.

Remember, if you keep thinking and acting in the way you've been thinking and acting, you'll keep getting what you've been getting.

So, get ready for increased success. Get mentally prepared to move ahead of the pack. Prepare your mind to enjoy a level of prosperity that you never thought you could attain.

I'm looking forward to being your partner in your expanded selling success.

One pound of learning requires ten pounds of common sense to apply it.

—PERSIAN PROVERB

1 Self-Understanding

Discovering Why You Sell What You Sell

THERE ARE FORCES DEEP WITHIN YOUR PSYCHE THAT ARE currently influencing at least 85 percent of your sales! You probably have no conscious awareness of them. And it's more than likely that what you've been taught about the causes of success in selling doesn't even come close to touching these forces.

Just think about that for a moment.

Marianne Szegedy Maszak reports in *U.S. News & World Report,* "According to cognitive neuroscientists, we are conscious of only about five percent of our cognitive activity, *so* most of our decisions, actions, emotions, and behavior depend on the ninety-five percent of brain activity that goes beyond our conscious awareness."

What's this got to do with your sales success? Everything. It literally holds the key to it.

Throughout this book I'll share a belief that selling is 15 percent knowledge, learned skills, or other intellectual factors; and the other 85 percent unconscious factors, such as attitudes, self-beliefs, feelings of worthiness, and other spiritual and emotional influences.

According to recent research I'm being a bit liberal—leaning too far to the intellectual, conscious knowledge side.

What Controls Your Ability to Sell?

What more than anything else is driving your current sales and career success? The economy? Your product or service? Your knowledge? Your support systems? Your CRM system? Your experience? Your company? Your compensation?

If you said, "Yes" to any of the above questions, I want to challenge you. It's my belief that a power much deeper than knowledge, outside circumstances, or conditions is driving your ability to sell. It's an inner power to which everyone has access, but few people actually discover and tap into.

In fact, I'll also say that your current level of sales success will not appreciatively change until you understand and plug into this unlimited source of energy. You'll do this as you internalize the actual success factors that I'll share with you in this book.

What is this deeper power? What are these success factors?

Your Sales Are Always Consistent with What You Deeply Believe to Be Possible for You to Sell

The odds are that you're currently selling exactly what you unconsciously believe you *should* be selling. These deep-seated self-estimates give the marching orders, and your habits, activities, and attitudes then, without questioning, carry them out.

Deep inside the recesses of your psychic caverns is written a description of what your achievement possibilities are, and the conscious part of you takes over, without challenges, and carries out these deep subconscious commands. Most often you'll assume that what you're currently selling is normal for you. So, without challenging your assumptions, you keep selling what you've been selling.

This explains why people plateau, fail, barely hang on, or succeed.

There's a profound part of you that over your lifetime has developed unconscious beliefs about:

- Who you are
- What you're capable of achieving
- What level of life rewards you deserve to enjoy.

This internal programming has been influenced by many factors. Among them are your parents, your early upbringing, and the love you experienced or didn't enjoy. You evaluate the whole of your life experiences and form strong inner perceptions.

All these perceptions were not based on truth, but what you *believed* to be the "truth." Whether your perceptions are true or false, if you believe them to be valid, they'll become your "realities" and then control all your actions, feelings, behavior, and abilities.

We all live out our lives, going with the flow of what we perceive to be our possibilities—rarely challenging these beliefs that aren't based on fact, but on our presumptions of what our realities are.

The Truth About You

The truth about you is that you have the inner power to achieve any goal you can *unconsciously accept* to be within your possibilities. If, after discovery, you aren't satisfied with your current views of your possibilities, you have the power to change them. I want to help you understand this truth in every chapter of this book. You won't understand it just because I say it to you; you'll only "get" it experientially by discovery. This won't happen because you read and know what I wrote; it will only occur as you practice the Action Guides I'll share with you.

Regardless of your current success, you'll be able to continue to climb as high as you unconsciously desire to go.

Let's take it a step further and begin to understand what this power is and where it resides within you.

You're Made Up of Three Parts

There are three distinct parts of the one you. The model on page 18 will help you understand your own makeup, as well as serve as a framework to change your current life circumstances into whole new realms of higher achievement.

The *intellectual* "I Think" is the logical, rational, knowledge part of you; the part that learns information, makes decisions, and chooses behaviors or actions. This part decides on and sets goals, but lacks the octane power to carry them out.

But there's more to us than this conscious, surface level.

The *emotional* "I Feel" is the part of you that experiences feelings and emotions. For no reason, you may feel down today, but yesterday you felt elated. Someone compliments you and you feel nice. A driver cuts you off

The Three Dimensions of Human Behavior

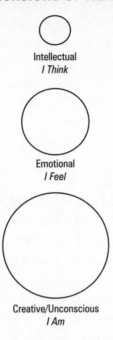

Intellectual
I Think

Emotional
I Feel

Creative/Unconscious
I Am

at an intersection and you suddenly feel angry. Try as you might, you can't logically understand the cause and effect of these mood differences.

Where do your feelings come from? What triggers them? Why can't you consciously change or even control them?

The *creative/unconscious* "I Am" is the spiritual dimension within you. Because of this connection with the Infinite it gives you access to unlimited power and energy—once you learn to access and tap into it. Tapping into this power usually involves paradoxical behaviors, ones that tend to conflict with our natural ego-focused thinking.

I'll explain these dimensions in more detail in a moment, but first let's understand a basic interaction of these parts.

The Interaction between Your "I Think" and Your "I Am"

Throughout your wide awake hours, your "I Think" is constantly interacting with your "I Am." These exchanges then trigger the emotions in your "I Feel," which then powerfully influence your external behaviors.

Notice the graphic on page 19.

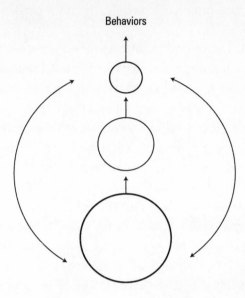

The interaction between your conscious "I Think" and your unconscious "I Am" automatically creates an emotion in your "I Feel." Your emotions are so powerful that they'll overrule the logic in your conscious "I Think" on average 85 percent of the time and motivate your external behaviors. Said another way, in a contest your conscious willpower, or discipline, is no match for your powerful emotions.

Here are a couple of examples.

Out of every 100 people who enter the life insurance industry, 11 will still be in it as they go into their fourth year. Just think of it: 89 percent don't make it.

Why?

It's not for lack of knowledge—whether of the product, the industry, or how to manage their activities. In fact, it's common for new agents to do well their first few months, only to fade away after the "old pros" educate them about what it takes to be successful, and what level of success is actually possible for them to achieve.

Every salesperson unconsciously answers these questions.

- "What does it take to be successful?"
- "Do I have what it takes to be successful?"

Often, because of personal beliefs, there's a conflict between their answers.

Certain sales skills are taught, and new agents say, "Man, if this is what it takes to make it, I probably can't do it." Their conscious understanding of "what it takes" interacts with their unconscious views of "what they have." A conflict then follows that triggers feelings of doubt, "call-reluctance," fear of the unknown, and other negatives.

These negative emotions are so powerful they'll usually obliterate their conscious desire to sell, causing them to mentally and emotionally shut down.

This inner tension defeated them before they even got started.

Your "I Think" can set goals, but if your "I Am" silently screams, "You're not capable of that," emotions of doubt and anxiety are triggered in your "I Feel." This conflict will often cripple your activity level and torpedo your ability to sell. Until the self-beliefs deep within your "I Am" change to fit the higher goals you set, you'll subconsciously throw all kinds of monkey wrenches into your mental and emotional machinery.

You'll "prove" to yourself and the world that selling isn't the business for you.

These conflicts intensify as managers put pressure on salespeople to "try harder," "make more calls," or "manage your time better." The more the pressure builds, the more clogged up and emotionally conflicted salespeople become. The inevitable then happens: they settle for low productivity, or go find another job they think might have less stress and conflict.

What are some answers to these challenges?

Sales Consistency

Here's my concept of Sales Consistency: People's sales are always consistent with their internal beliefs about:

1. Who they are
2. What's possible for them to sell or earn
3. What they deserve to have in life rewards.

One of our greatest emotional needs is for consistency. Predictability. Evenness. To know that future events aren't going to create waves that lap up over our chin line. One of the ways we manifest this need is to set goals, make decisions, and tackle problems that we're comfortable handling. Probably 85 percent of all salespeople do this without even knowing it.

There's an explanation for this emotional phenomenon. Years ago, Dr. Prescott Lecky, a Canadian educator, coined what he called the Theory of Self-Consistency. He developed this to help teachers enable students to learn more effectively. He theorized that our minds are organized systems of ideas, and all the ideas that belong to the system must seem to be consistent with each other.

He went on to state, "The center or nucleus of the mind is in the individual's conception of himself. If a new idea seems to be consistent with the ideas already present in the system, and particularly with the individual's conception of himself, it is accepted and assimilated easily. If it seems to be inconsistent, however, it meets resistance and is likely to be rejected."

What this means is that when the choices, decisions, or commitments you make with your "I Think" are in conflict with the beliefs, values, and self-image in your unconscious "I Am," a conflict occurs that inhibits your progress toward your goals. The concept of Sales Consistency leads us to understand:

When the choices, decisions, or commitments you make in your "I Think" are consistent with the beliefs, values, and self-image in your unconscious "I Am," a congruence occurs that accelerates your progress toward your goals.

But this phenomenon works both ways. It allows us to see things we perceive to be consistent with who we are, but it also blocks out anything that doesn't fit the personal, emotional, spiritual, or intellectual views we hold. There are two sides to the coin: one opens up the world to us, the other closes it off.

What We Don't *See*, We Don't *See*!

We all have a clear vision of the goals we presume to be within our reach, but anything outside them is well hidden by our emotional blind spots.

What we don't *unconsciously* see, we can't *consciously* see. It's as if it doesn't exist.

Did you ever begin to cross an intersection, after looking both ways, only to suddenly hear a motorist blare his horn at you, swerve to miss you, and give you a glare that would melt a freight train? Most of us have, haven't we? We understand these as physical, visual blind spots.

We also have mental, emotional, and spiritual blind spots. Lou Tice of the Pacific Institute, labels them *scotomas,* from the Latin for "blindness." They prevent us from seeing, discovering, or achieving the realities we could otherwise enjoy.

In short, we don't see what we don't see—we only see what we see.

A number of years ago a team of Stanford psychologists raised batches of kittens. Some were brought up to only see vertical lines; others were only allowed to see horizontal lines. Their brains actually rendered the world as vertical or horizontal. The vertical cats were incapable of seeing horizontal lines, and the horizontal cats were blinded to vertical lines.

All of us have scotomas—to various degrees. After having over 1.5 million people in my development courses, I'm convinced that 85 percent of all salespeople do not sell up to their potential. Including me!

Years ago when I lived in Texas, I was in the steam room of a YMCA when two men came in. I knew both of them. They didn't seem to notice me, since they were engaged in conversation. As I listened to them, I was struck with a paradox. Both were in the life insurance business, and I knew that they had about the same college education. As they talked, both seemed equally intelligent. If I hadn't known them, I absolutely wouldn't have known which one was the more successful.

But I did know them. I knew that one was failing in the business because he couldn't generate enough income to live on. The other was the legendary George Morris, who had been the top producer in The Prudential for more than twenty years. He probably earned a hundred times more income than the other man.

That experience shook me, and made me begin to look for deeper reasons why some people sell well and others don't. It took me way past the usual answers I'd previously had.

Now that you have a sketchy idea of the three dimensions of human behavior, and how they function to produce our outer behaviors, let's go deeper into understanding this wonder that we call the human mind. Because this book is about the Inner Game of Selling, let's lay a solid foundation for our knowledge, understanding, and action steps.

Functions of Your "I Think"

This conscious part directs your logic, rational thinking, choices, and decisions. Most of your education was directed to this dimension. The assumption was that if we're presented information we'll hear it, remember it, and practice it. Obviously, much of what we hear doesn't stay lodged in our "I Think," and, as I've mentioned, knowledge alone isn't all you need to sell well.

Your "I Think" gathers needed knowledge and information. With it you plan your calls or contacts. You make decisions about the best use of your time. You lay out client development strategies. You make reports, and revise your reports. Most of the formal training you've had was probably directed to the functions of your conscious "I Think."

You consciously choose words, actions, and sales behaviors. You choose your self-talk: what you say to yourself about yourself. With enough repetition and emotion, what you tell yourself finally reaches the deep beliefs in your "I Am." Yet you do have the conscious capacity to change the messages you express to yourself.

We get so accustomed to our own self-talk that we hardly notice it. They're just natural thoughts that jump from somewhere within us. A good way to understand your own self-talk is to listen to how other people express themselves. You'll hear statements like, "I'm always late." "I just can't lose weight." "Things like this are always happening to me." "I'm not sure that selling is the right career for me."

What do these statements have in common?

Right! They're negative.

As a salesperson you're constantly making choices and setting sales goals. Some of the decisions you make with your "I Think" find agreement with the beliefs in your "I Am," while others create conflict. The resulting interaction then influences appropriate emotions. Set a goal that you don't unconsciously believe to be possible for you, and the resulting interaction is one of conflict that triggers negative emotions of doubt, fear, and apprehension. Focus on creating value for customers, rather than just trying to sell them something, and this interacts with your inner values, creating confidence and inner harmony and releasing positive energy. As a result, you sell more.

Creating value for customers is helping them enjoy personal or corporate benefits or desired gratification. To the extent we help them solve their problems, reach their goals, or satisfy their unique needs, we serve them well.

Their satisfaction depends on the extent to which their benefits outweigh their cost. Notice this formula:

$$Value = Benefits - Cost$$

You make conscious choices about how you'll spend your time, either on result-producing or tension-relieving activities. You choose your environmental influences, where you go, from whom you'll learn, what you'll learn, and how you'll prepare yourself for your contacts.

Your conscious thinking processes are like the proverbial "tip of the iceberg." It's the small part that's visible, but it's being supported by a vast underwater system. It has little power that isn't supported by deeper dimensions within your "I Am."

Functions of Your "I Feel"

Your emotions are triggered by the choices or conscious thought processes that then interact with the deeper beliefs, values, and recordings within your "I Am."

Suppose you choose to tell a half-truth, because it momentarily helps you get by a sticky situation. Your choice collides with the values in your "I Am" to create an emotion of guilt. Since guilt doesn't feel good to you, it may cause you to choose different actions, behaviors, or responses to move past its pain.Some actions are healthy, others are unhealthy.

Your emotions are so powerful that they often overrule your logic or knowledge. You know that you should make a call on a difficult customer or prospect, but apprehension or fear of rejection sets in, stalling you and causing avoidance. Experience rejection on your last four contacts, and your emotions may send your confidence into hiding, and your view of your actual possibilities plummets. So, these negative emotions paralyze your behaviors.

I've seen many salespeople so racked with fear of rejection that they become emotionally frozen. Often, even knowing they have a family to feed and that selling is their only way to get money, they still don't make calls. In fact, many salespeople only produce at the level that feeds their basic subsistence. Unconsciously, they say, "How *little* do I have to sell to earn enough just to get by?"

Your emotions aren't under the direct control of your conscious willpower, discipline, or self-control. You can't change fear of rejection by saying to yourself, "Get over it." Or, "Work harder." Or, "Tough it out." You can, though, control negative, limiting emotions in *indirect* ways.

Since your emotions are so powerful in influencing your attitudes, actions, and behavior, you'll want to carefully develop ones that will fuel successful behaviors. I'll share strategies that will help you manufacture positive, healthy, success-producing emotions that will elevate your actual sales abilities.

Functions of Your "I Am"

This unconscious, spiritual dimension operates at many different levels within you. Among them are your:

- Self-Image—your unconscious belief of who you are, and what's possible for you to achieve.
- Values—the rules by which you run your life. How you measure right and wrong.
- Creative Mechanism—the ability to bring new ideas to the surface of your thinking. Your unconscious problem solver.
- Goal-Seeking Mechanism—the teleological, or self-guiding function that automatically steers you to your desired goals, corrects for feedback, and unveils options and opportunities to your conscious "I Think."

- Life Force—the physical and emotional thermostat that controls your heartbeat, lymphatic flow, and temperature.
- Spiritual Dimension—the intelligence within you that discerns things from a spiritual perspective, rather than from an ego-focused, human view.
- Past Recordings—all your past emotions, thoughts, experiences, and life perceptions that are silently stored deep within you.

Your "I Am" is the mission control of your whole being. It houses your belief boundaries, your "area-of-the-possible," and usually blocks your conscious "I Think" from seeing possibilities that are outside its belief system.

It's with your "I Think" that you set goals, but the beliefs in your "I Am" determine whether or not they'll be reached or abandoned. Carl Jung wrote, "Human behavior is influenced far more by instinct than generally supposed." He called these "subliminal self-perceptions." We all have them, and they reign supreme in influencing our external success.

The whole of your life experiences, thoughts, and perceptions are stored in the recordings of your "I Am." Because this is the spiritual part of you, it can't be measured by any logical or proven measurement. It contains spiritual wisdom as opposed to human wisdom. Jung calls it "the wisdom of the unconscious." He also introduced "the collective unconscious," by which we have access to the thoughts and wisdom of other people. This has several manifestations. I'll help you access the wisdom of other people in a later chapter.

M. Scott Peck points out in his classic work, *The Road Less Traveled,* that our unconscious is "wiser than we are about everything."

Hunches, intuition, and ideas bubble up from your "I Am" to your "I Think." Try as you might to remember a name, and it tends to bury itself more deeply. Forget about it, and when your conscious thoughts are a million miles away, the name suddenly pops into your mind. You shake your head and ask, "Where did that come from?"

You strive to solve a problem, only to become more confused and indecisive. You then wake up at 3 A.M. and the answer explodes in your mind. Any examination of this phenomenon leads us to conclude that something is going on deeply within us that we can't explain, or logically understand.

All creative people have either consciously or unconsciously discovered how to tap into this reservoir of unlimited power. Tragically, most people live and die having never known about it. When you seriously and consciously practice the Action Guides in this book, you'll learn to plug into this power. When you do, you'll experience an unleashing of personal energy and success that will drive you upward in life.

Intuitive Knowledge in Your "I Am"

Most of us possess a deep, unconscious sense of right and wrong. Intuitively, we know "right" attitudes and actions to take in our selling, as well as what's not "right." Quite often, traditional product-focused or transaction-focused selling takes us in the wrong direction.

Jung refers to this inner sense as the "Spirit of Wisdom." It resides in our "I Am" dimension, and without fanfare governs our emotions, unless they're completely sealed off. When our conscious choices, and their resulting behaviors, are congruent with this Spirit of Wisdom, or Spirit of Truth, we are emotionally and physically strengthened. When they're in conflict, we're physically, emotionally and spiritually weakened.

To "buy in" to these ideas, it's first necessary to understand that every thought or decision we have or make automatically produces a related emotion. The resulting emotion then creates positive or negative energy fields of various degrees of intensity. In short, our thoughts and intentions alter our behaviors, which bring on certain consequences.

Consider a couple of examples. When you honestly view and practice selling as a process of identifying and filling people's needs, and creating extra value for them above what they pay you, you "go strong." Both emotionally and physically. But when you believe and practice selling as doing or saying anything you have to do to convince someone to buy from you, you "go emotionally and physically weak."

This can be proven quite simply by a kinesiology experiment. Have a person of similar physical strength hold up his or her arm parallel to the ground. First test their arm strength by placing your hand on their wrist and gradually pulling it down. Don't jerk, just pull steadily down to get an idea of their natural strength.

Have them drop their arm, relax, and silently repeat with you, "I believe selling is a process of identifying and filling people's needs and creating value for them above what they pay me." Ask them to close their eyes and repeat this phrase several times, visualizing what it means. Test their arm strength again. You'll find them to be stronger than before.

Then ask them to relax and repeat several times this phrase, "I believe that selling is doing or saying anything I have to do or say just to make a sale," and focus on what it says. Ask them to continue thinking this thought and hold up their arm and resist you as much as possible, as you pull down on their arm. You'll find that they have little strength, and cannot resist you.

Conflicts or congruence between what we think, say, or do and the Spirit of Truth within us cause us to either "go weak" or "go strong." We react involuntarily to each.

Try this experiment with several people. Let them try it on you, and see if the results are not the same.

Common Choices We Make

Here are some common, everyday choices we make. Each one interacts with our inner "Knowledge of Truth" and manifests itself in our ability to sell. Each of these thoughts or intentions cause us to either go "strong" or "weak."

To "Go Weak"	To "Go Strong"
"It's all about me."	"It's all about you."
"I'm here for you to help me."	"I'm here to help you."
"I'm in it for what I get."	"I'm in it for the value I can create for you."
"I'm motivated by my need for money."	"I'm motivated to help you, knowing that I'll be compensated accordingly."

Throughout this book, I'll share with you success strategies that, when sincerely believed and practiced, will cause you to emotionally and physically "go strong." This will then be manifested in higher self-esteem, greater confidence, increased personal power, and higher physical energy.

You'll create stronger energy fields around you, and in a most mysterious way, your sales, customer relations, trust level, and personal feelings of worth will expand—causing you to sell on higher and higher levels.

What locks or unlocks the door to this power?

Inner Conflicts and Congruence

To access this deep dynamo of power, an intellectual, emotional, and spiritual harmony must come into congruence within you.

Here's another way the principle works: conflicts between your "I Think" and your "I Am" create blocks that keep the vault door to your potential power closed. Congruence between these two parts is the combination that swings the door open to reveal the riches inside.

I realize that what I'm presenting to you, as it relates to selling, may seem as foreign as the planet Mars. I can only say that the lack of understanding of these deep issues is precisely why most salespeople don't sell well—why they stay locked up with low productivity. All they know is that the ability to sell is an issue of knowing their products, or a few closing skills.

Unfortunately, they don't know what they could know.

Your Ability to Sell

You have, as a result of your life experiences, formed a system of beliefs and ideas deep within your "I Am." This has created boundaries so thick and impenetrable that you accept them as "fact" or "truth." And then you unconsciously set about to "prove" them to be correct. And prove them you do with your external actions and behaviors. All the motivation, skills training, and incentives in the world will be either short-lived or ineffective if they're inconsistent with your accepted "truth" about yourself and your possibilities.

The bottom line is, your ability to sell is an issue of your internal belief boundaries. You'll understand this on many different levels as you read and experience the ideas explored in each chapter. I'll keep mentioning this truth, and hope that each time you'll go deeper with your understanding of it.

We Unconsciously Seek Our Own Level

Referring back to the concept of Sales Consistency, let's emphasize that each one of us, after forming our own belief boundaries, consciously seeks experiences that support the beliefs and values in our "I Am." If I think I'm only capable of earning or selling a certain amount, I'll unconsciously seek out prospects or customers who will provide that level of sales. I will also only do the activities that produce the sales I believe I'm capable of selling.

Not only will I seek out these experiences, but I'll blindly avoid those possibilities that would bring me higher levels of sales or income. I'll almost always honor my internal comfort zones in my selling strategies. All you have to do is to observe a dozen salespeople to see this principle played out in actual behavior.

So strong is this inner belief mechanism that, in order to defend our own sense of integrity, we'll play all kinds of games to honor our self-chosen, yet hallowed beliefs. Here are a few of the "truths" that we tell ourselves to stay congruent with our limited inner beliefs about our boundaries.

"I'm working as hard as I can now."

"After all, there's more to life than making money, or work."

"Clients don't like to see me on Mondays or Fridays."

"I don't have as good a territory as . . ."

"I'm very happy the way I am."

Our self-limitations will be projected into our "realities" of today, and our actions, attitudes, and behaviors will be manufactured to carry them out, and prove them to be correct. The recordings on the inside end up played out on the outside.

Knowledge of Sales Skills Has Little to Do With Success

I want to emphasize again that your level of knowledge of sales skills has little to do with your actual sales success. Regardless of how much you know, when you form an inner belief about what the "norm" of possibility is for you, you'll bring all your *conscious and unconscious emotional powers to bear in proving it right.* You'll then stoutly resist any "evidence" to the contrary. You'll block out new ideas, incentives, and external motivations that don't fit your self-beliefs.

Unless our self-development is first aimed at helping us form new pictures of our real selves in our "I Am," we won't practice the skills that are taught to us. We're generally incapable of advanced learning until our unconscious conception of our self changes to fit the new information.

After a lot of experience with several hundred thousand people in our courses all over the world, I'm totally convinced that most salespeople have the abilities to be highly successful. The problem is that most never move out of their comfortable set of beliefs about *who they are* and *what's possible* for them to sell, and embrace the belief that *they deserve* to enjoy higher levels of success.

But there's an even deeper issue at stake here. I agree with the educator Prescott Lecky, who theorized that most people want to be perceived as intelligent and self-reliant, useful to others, willing to hold up their own end, and capable of making a contribution to others. So when a suggestion comes to them that they can be selling more, earning more, or being more successful, they unconsciously resist it, because accepting it would mean that their previous conception of who they are was, in fact, wrong.

Just think of it: we stoutly defend our vision of who we are, even to the extent of blocking our own growth and increased sales.

Here again is the concept of Sales Consistency. Our outer behaviors tend to carry out our inner beliefs, even when we are faced with evidence to the contrary.

The Breakthrough Process

Let me outline the process that will get you started in breaking through your current level of self-beliefs and consistently expanding your actual success boundaries.

1. *Become aware of your current behaviors.* Pay attention to the conscious choices you make or actions you take, or results you expect.
2. *Notice the attitudes or feelings that seem to influence these behaviors.* Ask yourself, "What's driving me to do this action or behavior? Is it

driven by confidence or fear? By the need to avoid stress, or the desire to succeed?"

3. *Attempt to connect these feelings and behavior with the unconscious beliefs that might be driving them.* It's likely that little will "pop out" to your consciousness at first. Just keep examining and looking for answers. Soon your "I Am" will send answers to your "I Think."

4. *Select new beliefs that you'd like to have embedded in your "I Am."* Through self-suggestion that I'll share with you in each chapter, you can begin to send those messages down inside yourself. You'll do that each week as you go through the chapters of this book.

5. *Have the courage to go through change, conflict, and ambiguity that comes as you grow and develop new beliefs.* You'll always go through these seemingly disruptive times until new beliefs have time to establish themselves deep within you.

A Quick Summary of Why You Sell What You Sell

1. Your sales are always consistent with what you deeply believe to be within your possibilities.

2. Your psyche is made up of three parts:
   - The "I Think"
   - The "I Feel"
   - The "I Am"

3. The programming in your "I Am" is the cause, and your actions, feelings, behavior, and abilities are the effects.

4. The interaction between your "I Think" and your "I Am" is triggering specific emotions in your "I Feel," which largely motivates your actions and behavior.

5. Without knowing it you seek the level of success that you feel to be within your actual abilities, and block out what seems to be outside your possibilities.

6. Your knowledge has little to do with your actual sales success; rather, what you believe to be "the truth about yourself" reigns supreme.

These are some of the main truths about you. They present a whole new paradigm of what it takes to be successful in selling. They take you much deeper than all the clichés, closing skills, manipulative gimmicks, and techniques that have confused, misled, and destroyed many salespeople's careers.

HOW TO GAIN THE MOST FROM THIS CHAPTER

Read and/or review this chapter several times this week. Underline points you want to remember or challenge. Make notes in the margins. Discuss the concepts with other salespeople who desire to learn and grow.

Carefully go through the five-step Breakthrough Process. Write the steps on a card so they'll be handy to refer to each day. At the end of each day, jot down what you've learned.

Get disturbed! Get upset at the false promises of surefire sales success you've been fed in the past. Begin to visualize yourself multiplying your sales, personal effectiveness, and client respect. Look around you and pick out things or circumstances you'd like to be enjoying, but have previously thought to be beyond your possibilities. Say to yourself, "Enjoying these is certainly within my possibilities. If other people can achieve these things, so can I!"

And several times this week, almost like a mantra, you can repeat this self-suggestion.

"I choose to take control of my success, to create increased value for people, and enjoy higher rewards."

Say and repeat this positive self-suggestion daily. When you say it, visualize the extra value you'll give to people, and internalize your sense of the rewards you'll enjoy when you do. It suggests a foundational belief that is necessary for increased success.

Remember: it's the programming in your "I Am" that's regulating your sales, income, or rewards. Your current level of programming has been developed largely by the self-suggestions you've programmed into it. You can change it the same way.

Your repetitive, emotional self-suggestions will eventually help you change the programming.

So, this week, define *who* you'll become, write it on a card, and repeat this vision of yourself over and over. Always *emotionalize* your self-suggestions by visualizing how you'll look, feel, and benefit when you become the person you were designed to be.

1 DISCOVERING WHY YOU SELL WHAT YOU SELL

Assessment

Please take a few moments and check off the number that best describes your present beliefs, boundaries, or behaviors. Use these descriptors as guidelines.

    5–Always true, without exception
    4–Mostly true
    3–True more often than not
    2–True only part of the time
    1–True only occasionally

1. Outside factors largely influence my sales.	5 4 3 2 1	1 2 3 4 5	1. My self-beliefs largely influence my sales.
2. Fear of rejection often hampers me.	5 4 3 2 1	1 2 3 4 5	2. I think about what I can do for people, not how they'll accept or reject me.
3. I hardly ever reach my sales goals.	5 4 3 2 1	1 2 3 4 5	3. I usually exceed my sales goals.
4. I really don't see how I can sell more than I'm now selling.	5 4 3 2 1	1 2 3 4 5	4. I study high achievers to get a picture of how I can reach higher goals.
5. When I'm not working I don't think about selling.	5 4 3 2 1	1 2 3 4 5	5. My creative mind is always revealing new ideas to me.
6. I'm working as hard as I can.	5 4 3 2 1	1 2 3 4 5	6. I'm constantly thinking about how I can make the best use of my time.
7. I never analyze my actual sales behaviors.	5 4 3 2 1	1 2 3 4 5	7. I'm always paying attention to my sales behaviors in order to be more effective.

8. I dread getting up in the morning.	5 4 3 2 1	1 2 3 4 5	8. I can't wait to start my day to see what opportunities will present themselves to me.
9. I tend to avoid stress-ful situations and problems.	5 4 3 2 1	1 2 3 4 5	9. I welcome challenges as a way to grow and become more suc-cessful.
10. Most of my self-suggestions are nega-tive and destructive.	5 4 3 2 1	1 2 3 4 5	10. Most of my self-suggestions are posi-tive and encouraging.

- Add up the numbers in the right-hand column. _____
- Add up the numbers in the left-hand column. _____
- Subtract the left-hand column total from the right-hand column total and score yourself. _____

SCORES:

40–50 You are very positive, open to learning, and have a high achievement drive.

30–39 You have a definitely positive orientation in your views and skills.

20–29 You have a moderately positive view of life and your ability to succeed.

10–19 You are on the right track and show exciting potential for improvement. There are still several areas that need attention. You still wrestle with fears and doubts.

0–9 You struggle with many issues of life and sales success. Some days you're positive, and others find you experiencing doubts and focusing more on negatives than positives.

Keeping Score—Chapter 1

Behavior that gets evaluated, gets improved.

On a scale of 1–10, please evaluate your performance of each of these parts of the Breakthrough Process.

	S	M	T	W	T	F	S
1. I became aware of my current behaviors.							
2. I noticed the attitudes or feelings that influenced these behaviors.							
3. I attempted to connect these feelings and behaviors with the unconscious beliefs that might be driving them.							
4. I selected new beliefs that I'd like to have embedded in my "I Am."							
5. I have the courage to go through change, conflict, and ambiguity.							
Total Each Day							

2 Boundaries

Examining Your Current Belief Boundaries

EACH OF US HAS OUR OWN UNIQUE, UNCONSCIOUS BELIEF boundaries.

They're self-imposed. Self-manufactured. Silently fabricated by our perceptions of the truth about ourselves. They're not actual truth, but figments of our own creations.

Without questioning their authenticity we live out their strict controls. They victimize us or elevate us. They predetermine our levels of sales success. We rarely challenge them.

But challenge them we must, if we're to reach the higher levels of success that we're capable of enjoying.

First, let's take a look at how some other people think and act.

World-Class High Achievers

The average retail salesperson for new cars sells around eight vehicles a month. Stars sell around fifteen and rare superstars average twenty. When I spent a day in the late 1980s with Larry Merritt of Tom Jumper Chevrolet in the Atlanta metro area, he had just gone into the *Guinness Book of World Records* for having sold twelve thousand cars in his career. He averaged sixty retail units a month for a twenty-year period.

Yes, *sixty . . . per month . . . for twenty years!*

Larry and all the other salespeople at his dealership had just completed our Integrity Selling course when I heard of him. So I wanted to spend a day with him to see who this person was who could perform sales miracles.

35

When I met him he looked like the man-next-door in a moderate, family-oriented neighborhood. Modest dress, quiet demeanor, friendly—a sincere, nice man. Nothing that I expected, but like someone you'd see at church, or a Lions Club, or at a PTA meeting.

What was his secret? I wanted to know.

I found out that he didn't have a secret. No tricky closes. No hype or magic formula. No *open sesame* that took him to the heights he'd attained. He just did simple things. His son assisted him and they had a card file (before the days of personal computers) on every customer who'd bought a car from him. He knew their birth dates, anniversary dates, children's names and ages, and special interests.

Larry spent at least two hours each day writing notes to his customers on their special occasions. He looked for events or achievements they were involved in, and wrote them a congratulatory note. When he wasn't writing notes, or with customers, he called them to see how they were doing. He sent out periodic mailings. He never waited around the showroom, but had his customers come to his office.

His customers became his associates, sending their friends and family to him. When he sold to their referrals he'd send his customers flowers or other gifts of thanks.

After visiting with him I asked myself the obvious question, "What is he doing that other salespeople *couldn't* do?" The answer was, "Nothing!" Anyone could do the simple activities that he did. Simple, but with extraordinary results.

Then why wasn't every salesperson selling on this level?

Could it have anything to do with their belief boundaries? With their values? Their view of selling? Of their view of their abilities?

The difference could have been as simple as:

- They saw themselves as selling cars.
- Larry saw himself as serving both his customers and dealership.

Could it really be that simple?

Ever since then, when I drive by a car dealership and see salespeople bunched together like hawks, ready to pounce on anyone with the courage to walk up to them, I think of Larry, and how he did the business so differently.

I Met a Legend

Years ago, I met Elmer Leterman, then a legend in the life insurance business. I was at the beginning of my career; he was near the end of his. I'll never forget him. His story became an ongoing symbol of selling success—one I would reflect upon many times over the years.

I was in The Plaza hotel in New York City, looking through a book rack on the newsstand. I saw one of his books and picked it up. As I was looking through it, a voice behind me said, "If you'll buy it, I'll sign it for you." I looked around and Elmer introduced himself to me.

I bought the book, *Personal Power Through Creative Selling*. He autographed it, and invited me to have lunch with him and his wife in the Palm Court.

Elmer had sold more life insurance than anyone else in the history of the business. He sold more than most companies did. He sold over $1 million his first week! That was in the late 1920s, and would probably convert to $25 million in today's market.

I was curious to know how he could achieve the sales goals he had met. I expected to hear about magical sales skills, but what I found out was much different.

Elmer told me that he didn't have the greatest knowledge of the industry, but did have fifteen Charted Life Underwriters back in his office who knew everything about it. He explained that he had a table reserved at the Four Seasons restaurant, and invited six guests to join him for lunch five days a week. He'd invite business people, sports figures, show business people, writers, news people, and others to join him. He never discussed his business; his only objective was to help his guests know one another. He'd then put them on his list and mail ideas to them.

Elmer insured the famous Betty Grable's legs, and the great comedian Jimmy Durante's nose. He insured the legendary heavyweight fighter Jack Dempsey. In 1930, in the height of the Great Depression, he sold $58 million worth of insurance for John Hancock alone. Incredible!

He had a full-time assistant whose only job was to send books, articles, and referrals to people whom he'd met. He spent the big part of his time developing relationships, and obviously the unerring Law of Reciprocity worked for him.

Something in his life had convinced him that he could be successful on a higher level than anyone had ever reached before. Even during some of the most difficult economic times in modern history, he looked at the world and saw abundance. Others saw only scarcity.

Elmer was famous for telling people, "Only one thing can limit your achievements and success. That is yourself."

Bear in mind the bigger story here: Elmer's belief boundaries were so large that they led him to discover a different way to sell life insurance.

The single thing he had in common with all other salespeople was that his sales were consistent with his deep-belief boundaries. He believed he could sell on this high level, so his Creative Mechanism found a way for him to do it.

This is true of you, too! Your inner Creative Mechanism controls your sales to be consistent with your inner belief boundaries. Your sales only significantly change when your unconscious boundaries change.

How Were They Able to Do This?

What drove these two superstars of different generations? What caused them to reject the ordinary and discover a way to become extraordinary? How had they established such huge boundaries?

Elmer Leterman seemed to have a huge need for social acceptance. My relationship with him convinced me that he just wanted people to like him.

He carried a stack of folded copies of letters that famous people had sent him. A few minutes after I met him he pulled this stack, about an inch think, from his coat pocket and peeled out three or four different copies and gave them to me, silently waiting for me to read them. When I did, and complimented him, he smiled broadly, as if this was the first time anyone had done it.

Larry Merritt seemed to have no need for personal recognition, at least as far as I could tell. Nothing in his dress, office environment, or speech indicated that he had this need. He seemed to have an honest, sincere need to help people.

"I'm here to serve my customers and my dealership," was his explanation to me.

I'll make a guess and say that Elmer Leterman unconsciously defined the level of success he'd need in order to enjoy the lifestyle he most wanted, and that motivated him. Larry Merritt saw that he'd have to sell sixty cars each month in order to help the number of people he wanted to help.

Consider these two statements and you'll see a common thread. Both unconsciously viewed the *kind* and *level* of rewards they wanted to enjoy, and their answer was, "Okay, if this is the level of rewards I want, here's how much I'll have to sell and/or earn in order to enjoy it. To do this, here is the number of people I must help. And . . . here's the process I've creatively figured out to help this many people, so I can sell this much."

Reflect for a moment on this last thought, and then apply it to your sales role. While many people use their Creative Mechanism for survival; these two superstars chose to use it to achieve abundance. They knew that this was a choice they could make. Most people today don't know this. But you will . . . after you finish this book.

Your Belief Boundaries

Each of us has developed unique unconscious beliefs about our abilities and possibilities. Without much conscious thought we decide and live out our answers to these questions:

- What's possible for me to sell?
- What's possible for me to earn?
- What size sales are possible for me to make?
- What level of people am I able to call on?
- What kind of home is possible for me to live in?
- How much money am I able to save and invest?
- What places can I afford to go?
- What kind of clothes am I able to wear?
- What kind of education can I give my children?
- What rewards and advantages am I able to give my family?
- What level of value can I create for people?

As I've mentioned before, our answers may or may not be based on truth, but we treat them as if they are. They've become our perceived "realities."

What are some of your belief boundaries? What's possible for you, and what's not possible? What are *your* "perceived realities"? Let's think of some beliefs that influence these boundaries.

Your Definition of Selling

I define selling as a process of identifying and satisfying people's wants or needs. It's creating extra value for them above the price they pay you for it. Please stop and read this definition again.

Do you agree with it? No, not just mentally giving assent to it, but believing it viscerally down deep in your gut! But even more than that—does this describe how you currently sell?

Frankly, I'll bet that this isn't the way you've been trained to sell. It isn't if you've been taught selling skills as a way to convince or persuade people to buy what you're selling.

Think of these questions as you determine how you sell.

1. Do you prospect by asking yourself, "Who can I sell something to?" Or, do you ask, "Who might have a need, want, problem, or challenge I can help fill, satisfy, or solve?"
2. Do you approach people with the intent of selling them something, or with the intent of first gaining trust and rapport with them?
3. After gaining trust and rapport do you tell them about your product or service, or do you ask questions to determine whether they have needs you can help them fill?
4. Do you expect people to buy what you're selling because they understand its features, advantages, and benefits, or to make that decision because your offering will help them reach their individual goals?
5. After people understand your product or service features, do you attempt to close them, or do you draw them out and make sure your solution is a fit?
6. Do you view negotiation as a process of convincing people to see things your way, or do you view it as a process of seeing things their way? Do you view it as working out problems that keep people from buying—when they want to buy?
7. Do you believe that closing is getting someone to do what *you* want

them to do, or do you view it as a step they want to take because of the benefits they'll enjoy?

How you honestly answer these questions will determine your actual view of selling. Your real beliefs will then impact your ability to sell. Your deepest intent will manifest itself in your behaviors.

A healthy, value-focused view of selling causes an emotional congruence within you, giving you energy, confidence, and a free-flowing pervasive sense that what you're doing is right, good, and healthy.

The Value You Create for Clients

After you adopt a positive view of successful client-focused selling, you'll want to then detail the quantity and quality of value you bring to people. As you consciously do this you'll place yourself in a rare minority of other salespeople. This will cause you to jump miles ahead of your competitors, who are still focused on what the customer can do for them, not what they can do for customers.

Where most salespeople focus on selling their product or service, you can differentiate yourself by stressing what your product or service will do for your customers. You'll stand out when you concentrate on the value they'll enjoy because of what you sell them.

See the difference? It's huge!

Here's the question you can ask each day: "What end-result benefits can I help people enjoy with my products or services?" How you answer it with your actions can change your success level.

What mind-set drives this thinking?

Your Abundance Mentality Level

Most highly productive people have what I'll call *an abundance mentality*. Simply stated, they look at the world and see abundance rather than scarcity.

I've shared the following process with many salespeople. When they do it daily a transformation happens in their thinking. A stronger abundance mentality is generated within them.

This emotional preparation process only takes a few minutes. I've seen it double and triple people's sales, as well as save many people who were about to quit or be terminated. I've seen people earning over 1 million dollars per year begin it and go on to enjoy significant increases.

Developing an Abundance Mentality

1. Tomorrow's date
2. Who will I contact tomorrow?
3. What extra value might I create for them?
4. How might they feel when I give them extra value?
5. How will I feel when I give them extra value?

At the end of each day take five to ten minutes and write out this process on a card or a sheet of paper, filling in some of the names, extra value, and feelings of your customers and yourself. Doing it in your own handwriting will get you closer to your emotions. Your "I Am" will work on it during the night. Soon you'll establish new belief boundaries of abundance in your "I Am." You'll begin to develop powerful, emotional beliefs like:

- I bring value to people above what they pay me.
- They feel good about my doing this.
- I feel good about doing this, and it gives me tremendous confidence.
- I have a totally positive view of selling and view it as an honorable profession.
- I have a totally positive view of me and my possibilities for success.
- I focus daily on prosperity and abundance.

This activity is mental, emotional, and spiritual dynamite. You can't possibly imagine its power until you've done it for several weeks. I challenge you to expand your success by doing this five-minute activity daily. Remember, it has more power if you'll do it at the end of your workday or evening. That way your powerful Creative Mechanism will work on it as you sleep.

You're probably asking the same question that our course participants ask: "How long and how often should I actually keep writing it out on a card?"

My answer is, "Only as long as you want to continue increasing your sales, personal confidence, and success!" When you're selling as much as you ever want to sell, or are earning as much as you ever want to earn—stop doing it. Until then, keep writing it out each day.

Rewards You Feel You Deserve to Enjoy for the Value You Create

Now we're getting down close to the deepest driver of your sales success. Far down in the vaults of your "I Am" you've unconsciously reached the conclusion, "How worthy am I?" You've also silently answered the question, "What level of success, rewards, or compensation do I deserve to enjoy?"

Right or wrong, these deep beliefs rule your behaviors from a powerful throne well concealed from your conscious ability to comprehend. They've been formed so they're the product of and consistent with your self-esteem. They become one of your strongest self-motivators.

While you'll never fully understand what these beliefs are, you can begin to gain insights into them by carefully observing your external behaviors and expectations. They give you daily clues, because your inner beliefs directly drive your external behaviors. So, working backward, you can begin to identify your unconscious beliefs.

As we've grown up all of us have silently answered the questions, "How valuable am I? How capable am I? How loved am I?" Our perceptions of our life experiences have then caused us to form our own answers. It's thought that, unless we've worked to change it, two-thirds of our self-esteem level was formed by the time we were three years old. We develop this emotional and physical set-point and carry it with us for the rest of our lives, unless we work at resetting it.

I have a good friend, a very nice, sincere person who loves his family and honestly wants to provide for them the best he can. He was severely verbally and physically abused by his father when growing up. He has a very high level of achievement drive and skills, while at the same time having the carryover feelings of his youth when his father constantly told him how worthless he was.

The conflict within him is enormous. He did extremely well his first year or so in selling, only to plummet after that. In talking to him, it became obvious to me that deep down in his "I Am" he didn't feel worthy of that level of success. It was like he was screaming to himself, "You don't deserve this amount of success." To prove this his sales hit bottom the next two or three years, as he barely hung on.

It's my opinion that he unconsciously punished himself for doing better than he felt he deserved to do.

How Deserving of Higher Success Levels Do You Feel?

What rewards do you feel worthy of receiving? What don't you feel you deserve to enjoy?

As I've listened to people in our development courses, many have consciously and unconsciously revealed deep inner conflicts that keep them from enjoying high success. I've heard many people talk about "bad" things they've done in their lives, for which they've been unable to forgive themselves. So as punishment, they unconsciously fail at jobs.

I've seen how negative emotions of anger, guilt, and remorse rob people of the ability to feel good about success. In a real sense, we all regulate our external success to conform to our internal feelings of worth. If things seem to be going better than we expect, we have the power to regulate them downward to fit our inner sense of value. Or vice versa: our feelings of worthiness can help pull us out of slumps.

It's in this area that we can learn from different disciplines.

Herbert Benson, a professor at Harvard Medical School, wrote in his excellent book *Timeless Healing* (Scribner, 1996), "More and more, I became convinced that our bodies are wired to benefit from exercising not only our muscles but our rich inner human core—our beliefs, values, thoughts, and feelings."

He went on, "And I could not shake the sense I had that the human mind—and the beliefs we so often associate with the human soul—had physical manifestations."

Benson also makes the point: "Our brains are wired for beliefs and expectations. When activated, the body can respond as if the belief were a reality, producing deafness, or thirst, health or illness."

In a related vein, William James once wrote that our emotions have a motor effect. They translate themselves into outer behaviors. They create their own realities.

Our Need to Deal with Negative Emotions

To the extent we attempt to live by moral or spiritual codes of conduct but miss the mark, or have no spiritual resources guiding us, we suffer negative emotions of guilt, remorse, and even self-loathing. But who of us is perfect?

In deeper ways I'm convinced that the ability to sell is closely akin to a spiritual one. Negative emotions—guilt, remorse, fear, anxiety—destroy physical energy, emotional confidence, and even a deeper spiritual sense of significance. How do you handle these destructive emotions? Are you able to forgive yourself in a creative way? What spiritual resources do you call on?

What does this have to do with selling, anyway? This warm-and-fuzzy, spiritual stuff?

Everything. Because it deeply influences how we see ourselves in our innermost depths.

Negative emotions are handled in paradoxical ways. Direct attempts to "not worry," or "get over guilt," or "just move past your anger," are usually compounded as we attack them directly. We must have more indirect ways to deal with them, such as prayer, meditation, and physical exercise. We need to forgive others for hurts and insults they've inflicted on us, and ask others to forgive us for the same.

Since your ability to sustain high-level selling success is more an issue of healthy self-image than anything else, the ability to deal with negative, destructive emotions is critical.

Destructive emotions can damage your self-esteem, which then cripples your ability to sell. Positive emotions can insulate you from the ravages of fear, worry, anxiety, and all their emotional cousins.

Remember, it's an inner game. But what causes these deep beliefs?

Influences upon Your Self-Beliefs

Many factors have influenced your current self-esteem or belief boundaries. A few are your:

Parents' beliefs

Early nurturing or parental love

Early environment

Perceived past success or failures

Teachers' messages

Mentors or managers

Spouses or friends

Response to life's ups and downs

Sibling order

Spiritual underpinnings

Perception of past successes or failures

Belief of the level that your customers value you

Belief of the value you create for customers

There are more influences; these are sufficient to think about here. My point is that we have all kinds of experiences as we go through life, and we tend to unconsciously evaluate how we did in each one. The cumulative effect then makes up our individual belief boundaries.

Your Area-of-the-Possible

You have two well-defined inner boundaries: your *area-of-the-possible,* and your *area-of-the-impossible.*

With your actions, behavior, skills, and abilities you answer two questions:

1. *"What's possible for me to sell and earn?"*
2. *"What's impossible for me to sell and earn?"*

Your answers then determine your area-of-the-possible, as well as your area-of-the-impossible.

Look at it like in the graphic on page 49.

The wall that divides these two beliefs is so tall and thick that it seems impregnable. It keeps us from seeing or believing what's on the other side, or from even considering the possibility that we could actually get there.

Consider your past three years' sales and/or income. What's the aver-

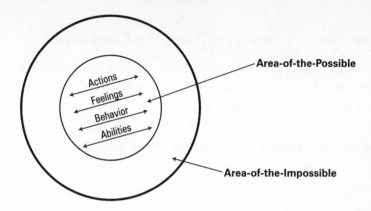

age per year? If you're like most other salespeople, the last three years have been pretty level. The reason is because that's what you unconsciously expected to earn. Chances are that's what you *had* to earn in order to pay your bills and live on the level where you expected to live.

But take a look around you at other salespeople—either in your own organization or others. Are there people selling or earning two, three, or four times what your last three years' average was? How were they able to do this? Are they two, three, four times as intelligent as you? Or have more product knowledge? Or work many more hours than you? Or have made more contacts or calls than you?

Probably not.

Then let me ask you another question: "What level of sales and/or income is *impossible* for you to achieve?"

Before you answer, let me ask it differently: "Think about your fantasy home for a moment. Imagine that it comes with gardeners, security people, and has a five-car garage with three vintage cars alongside your new Mercedes S Model and Porsche 911. To what extent do you see yourself being capable of owning these?"

Does this possibility move into the realm of your area-of-the-impossible?

Okay, relax. I'm not picking on you, because I have the same problem. Everyone does to one degree or another. My area-of-the-impossible might be smaller or larger than yours, but we all have them. And pardon me if I sound too materialistic. I'm only using tangible examples to make my points.

Other People Cause Us to Define Our Boundaries

I had a very critical, abusive father, who rarely missed a chance to put me down, make fun of me, or show his displeasure with me. I don't remember a single time that he ever complimented or encouraged me, or gave me a positive response. So, guess what? I grew up with very low self-esteem, inwardly thinking that I deserved little in the way of life's rewards, because he had convinced me that this was my reality.

My father was a very low achiever and I was always embarrassed about our level of living. Most of my high school years I slept on a small rollaway bed in our tiny kitchen. I didn't want any of the kids at school to know where I lived. I never took any friends home with me.

The messages I got from my father were, "Nothing you ever do is right. We don't have much, and you shouldn't expect much, because you don't deserve much."

I rebelled against him by going to church, working my way through college, then attempting to prove him wrong by becoming far more successful than he ever was. Of course, I didn't understand all this until years later, when I gained the insight to see the cause and effect that was at play in my life.

We Tend to Live Out Our Inner Beliefs

When I first began to conduct personal growth courses years ago, I expected to have significant results in the lives of my participants, but to be paid little. I had people tell me that they'd doubled their income as a result of my course. I can remember having millionaires as participants, excitedly telling me what they'd learned and gained, while I myself didn't have two nickels to rub together.

Something was wrong with that picture, but I didn't see it at the time, because what I was charging was all I thought *I* was worth. Not what *my course* was worth, but what *I* was worth. I thought my courses were worth a lot to my participants, but I wasn't convinced that I should be compensated accordingly.

In fact, I proudly told people that I wasn't in it for the money.

How blind I was. How I robbed myself and my family of what should have been ours. I hadn't accepted the law of balance that says:

> If I create high value for others, I should
> be compensated accordingly.

One day it dawned on me that it was my own poverty consciousness, or low expectations of reward, that had me out of balance. Not only did I owe it to people in my courses to help them enjoy greater personal and organizational prosperity, but I also owed it to myself and my family to allow them to pay me consistently with the value I'd helped them enjoy.

We're Blinded to Higher or Lower Levels

The futurist Joel Barker calls this phenomenon *Paradigm Paralysis*. Whatever our current level of success, we accept it as "normal" and so continue with the activities, actions, and behavior that keep us at that point.

In a sense, we're blinded to either higher or lower levels of achievement. We don't really, deep down, consider them "possible." We may even stoutly resist effort, help, information, or new skills that would tend to move us off our current level. We even unconsciously select people and circumstances to help keep us where we are.

Anytime we move ahead of where we deeply believe we should be, we experience strange, uncomfortable new feelings; these sensations or perceived threats then push us right back to where we think "normal" is. Since our greatest emotional needs include consistency, order, and a stressless, predictable life, we tend not to launch into less certain waters but rather stay in our own little pool where we know what the temperature and depth is.

Do you play golf? If you do, have you ever been three or four strokes ahead of your average score going into the fifteenth hole? After you realized this, what happened on the rest of the holes? If you're like most people you thought, "Oh no, I shouldn't be doing this well. I'm playing above my game." So for the rest of the holes you "proved" it by getting double bogeys and ended up scoring at what your "normal" game is.

What happened?

Internal Conflicts Either Motivate or Demoralize Us

Inner conflicts can arise anytime we catch ourselves performing on a different level than our perceived norm. We feel congruent when acting in ways that fit our beliefs of what we *should* be doing.

Change and personal growth can create internal conflict—created by a dissonance between what we want to happen and what is actually happening. This discomfort can motivate us or stall us out, depending on how we view it.

Conflict can either be positive or negative. Positive conflict creatively affects us, causing us to look for better ways to get things done or to reach goals. It causes enthusiasm, hope, and other expansive emotions. It energizes our thoughts, feelings, and bodies.

Negative conflict can jam our creative machinery and cause us to shut down and focus on survival goals. This triggers fear, anxiety, worry, and a host of other destructive emotions. It diminishes energy and enthusiasm.

In the real world, who hasn't felt the trauma of unmet quotas, of pressure to sell more, while still having to pay the bills?

Negative Conflict

Many salespeople experience negative conflict. Their chief motivation is basic survival, and they find it very difficult to move off that focus because it's so self-reinforcing. This causes them to release destructive energy. The longer they stay in this state, the more difficult it is to break out of it.

Negative conflict is associated with these states of mind, these choices and values:

- *I need to sell you something for my benefit.*
- *I'm totally focused on how I'm going to survive, rather than on how I can help you.*
- *I'll say or do anything just to make a sale.*
- *My whole interest is in what you can do for me.*
- *I'm so accustomed to just barely scraping by financially, this is all I expect.*

The conflict comes when you make these choices with your "I Think" and they then interact with the truth, wisdom, and values in your "I Am." The resulting interactions cause negative emotions in your "I Feel." These emotions of guilt, remorse, or "I'm not proud of me for doing this" then debilitate, de-energize, and discourage you.

Positive Conflict

Positive conflict, on the other hand, energizes and creatively motivates you. It's healthy. It uplifts and enables you. You feel good about who you are and wholesome about what you do. You can stand tall and look people in their eyes with confidence and self-respect.

Positive conflict is triggered by these attitudes, values, or behaviors:

- *I need to create as much value for you as I can.*
- *I would never try to sell you something unless it's the best solution for you.*
- *I owe it to my company to be as productive as possible.*
- *I am constantly searching for ways to help more people.*
- *I never worry about earning income, because I know it comes to me in large amounts when I create high value for customers.*

This conflict is driven by the need to be the best steward of our time, talents, and money as possible.

The Action Guides and self-suggestions I prescribe in this book are all designed to help you develop healthy conflict. I call it *creative dissatisfaction.* This is the attitude that says, "I'm thankful for who l am and what I have, and how I'm able to help people. I have a responsibility to create as much value for people as I can; and, since I know I'll be rewarded according to the value I create, I expect to enjoy high rewards."

It's the self-talk that says, "I look for new, creative ways to give extra value to customers. And I know that when I look, I'll find them."

Here's a process you can use to create positive conflict within yourself.

Creating Positive Conflict

1. With your conscious "I Think," define the quantity and quality of extra value you want to create for your clients, customers, patients, or members.
2. Define the level of rewards you'll earn when this happens.

3. When this is your focus, the values in your "I Am" will respond, "This is the right focus, and you should be rewarded according to the value you create."

4. This goal/values congruence will then trigger positive emotions in your "I Feel" by giving you more energy, achievement drive, and confidence.

Paradoxically, when you focus on the value you can create for others, rather than just what you can sell them, you'll feel clean, worthwhile, and deserving. This mind-set communicates strong character, integrity, and professionalism, which triggers a reciprocal value that comes back to you. Positive conflict is created when the value you'd like to be creating for customers is greater than what you're now doing.

So, what will you do to create positive conflict?

1. Set goals to create greater value for customers.

2. Expect to be awarded consistent with the value you create.

HOW TO GAIN THE MOST FROM THIS CHAPTER

I have designed this chapter to help you understand and challenge your current belief boundaries.

Whatever your beliefs, they've been developed over your lifetime and powerfully—more than just about anything else—control your ability to sell.

Please read and review this chapter and ask yourself these questions.

1. *What is my current belief level about:*
   - *My definition of selling?*
   - *The value I create for people?*
   - *My abundance mentality?*
   - *The rewards I feel I deserve to enjoy for the value I create?*
2. *How are these beliefs influencing my current ability to sell and earn?*
3. *What's the gap between my current ability to sell and earn, and what I would like to be selling and earning?*
4. *What inner beliefs do I need to have to produce at this increased level?*
5. *How do I deal with the destructive emotions of guilt, remorse, fear, or anxiety?*

Sometime this week, observe the behaviors, attitudes, and results of different salespeople. Try to understand how each one's circumstances might give a clue to his or her belief boundaries.

And finally, use this self-suggestion, over and over, to drill into your unconscious "I Am."

"I see abundance everywhere, and I allow myself to partake in it."

Repeat this to yourself each day and visualize the abundance you'll help create for your customers and your organization, along with the rewards you'll enjoy in return. Emotionalize it by thinking about the respect you'll receive from customers and your associates, the confidence you'll feel within yourself, and the actual tangible rewards you'll experience.

The more your "I Am" accepts this message, the more confidence, energy, and personal power you'll enjoy.

As your inner belief boundaries continually expand, new levels of sales success will rush in to fill the newly created space.

2 EXAMINING YOUR CURRENT BELIEF BOUNDARIES

Assessment

Please take a few moments and check off the number that best describes your present beliefs, boundaries, or behaviors. Use these descriptors as guidelines.

5–Always true, without exception
4–Mostly true
3–True more often than not
2–True only part of the time
1–True only occasionally

1. I feel definite limitations in what I can sell.	5 4 3 2 1	1 2 3 4 5	1. I think of possibilities to increase sales, rather than limitations.

	5 4 3 2 1	1 2 3 4 5	
2. I sell just enough to keep my job.	5 4 3 2 1	1 2 3 4 5	2. I set stretch sales goals, and then figure out how I can reach them.
3. I often ask myself, "Who can I sell something to?"	5 4 3 2 1	1 2 3 4 5	3. I usually ask myself, "Who has a need I can help them satisfy?"
4. I spend most of my contact time explaining my product or service.	5 4 3 2 1	1 2 3 4 5	4. I never talk about my product or service until a customer admits a need, a desire for a solution, and is willing to talk to me about it.
5. I usually operate on a survival level.	5 4 3 2 1	1 2 3 4 5	5. I focus on the abundance that's available to me.
6. I really don't believe I can make a high enough income in selling.	5 4 3 2 1	1 2 3 4 5	6. I feel worthy of high success levels, because I create high value for people.
7. My parent(s) put me down and discouraged me often.	5 4 3 2 1	1 2 3 4 5	7. My parent(s) told me that I can do anything I really want to do.
8. I've had more failures than successes in life.	5 4 3 2 1	1 2 3 4 5	8. I've had more successes than failures in life.
9. My view of selling conflicts with my values or spiritual beliefs.	5 4 3 2 1	1 2 3 4 5	9. My view of selling is quite congruent with my values or spiritual beliefs.
10. I usually think about how I'm going to benefit from my selling.	5 4 3 2 1	1 2 3 4 5	10. I usually think about how my customers will benefit from my selling.

- Add up the numbers in the right-hand column.   _____
- Add up the numbers in the left-hand column.   _____
- Subtract the left-hand column total from the right-hand column total and score yourself.   _____

Assessments scoring guide is on page 35.

Keeping Score—Chapter 2

Behavior that gets evaluated, gets improved.

On a scale of 1–10, please evaluate your performance of each of these parts of the Breakthrough Process.

	S	M	T	W	T	F	S
1. I defined the quantity and quality of extra value I'll create for people.							
2. I defined the level of rewards I'll earn when this happens.							
3. I told myself, "This is the right focus. I should be rewarded according to the value I create."							
4. I expected to have more energy, achievement drive, and confidence because of this belief.							
Total Each Day							

3 Breakthrough

Shattering Blockages of Your Success

NOT LONG AGO I BEGAN A SPEECH TO ABOUT 250 COLDWELL Banker managers in Florida by asking, "How many of you are currently on a plateau?"

Three hands went up; mine was one of them.

Then I asked, "Would everyone please hold up your hands, and keep them up when I ask the next question?" Then I asked, "How many of you are currently on a plateau?"

Everyone looked from right to left and some nervous laughter broke out. They weren't sure whether I was playing games or where I was going with them.

I went on, "It's my belief that every one of us is currently on a plateau, and all of your agents are also. We're currently performing consistently with strong inner beliefs about what's possible for us to sell or produce. Unless we choose to *think, believe,* and *act* in expanded ways, today and every day thereafter, we'll keep getting pretty much the same results that we've been getting."

I believe this.

Most salespeople have mental, emotional, or spiritual blockages that keep us performing on about the same level as we've been performing. Not only this, but we often unconsciously resist any suggestion that we could be selling much more than we currently are.

As I've said before, these blocks are largely self-imposed. They're our perception of "truth." Not actual truth, but they nonetheless become almost impenetrable, and difficult to scale.

Here's why.

Our Blocks Serve Some Inner Need

Each of our boundaries has been established because it generally serves some deep need we have. The inner need to reward or punish ourselves. To avoid pain or enjoy gain. To live up to our own or others' expectations of us. To be true to our own self-image. To conform to our self-perceived "norm." To gain approval from others. To yield to the controlling beliefs of others. To carry out acquired cultural or religious beliefs.

You'll discover as you work through this chapter, and as you seek to move beyond your current boundaries, that there's a reason why you unconsciously or consciously need to hang on to old perceptions. In some way your need to stay within your current level of performance is serving your self-beliefs or other influences in your life. As you understand this, you'll see why we resist accepting higher possibilities for our success, because this could:

1. Silently say that we aren't okay now.
2. Reveal that we avoid personal growth, because it might place new responsibility and stress on us, which we'd rather avoid.
3. Cause us to admit that we feel powerless to actually change our current situation.
4. Reveal that old dogmas, handed-down beliefs or values, or other people's beliefs weren't hallowed after all.

Since none of us have reached perfection yet, we all get locked into limited thinking.

If you agree with me, and are open to self-examination, then this will come as a breath of new thought—and create an inner disturbance, which can become very helpful and creative.

Purpose of This Chapter

I am challenging you by asking lots of questions about your current situation. I'm assuming that you have a high desire to expand your sales, income, and general life success, and that you're willing to go through an uncomfortable yet exhilarating self-analysis and growth experience that must precede your expanded area-of-the-possible.

So, my plan is to help you:

1. Understand the reality of plateaus and blockages
2. Discover your current blockages (remember, we all have them)
3. Identify why you have a need to hang on to them
4. Learn a process for releasing and moving through them.

Imagine what could happen in your life if you successfully completed these four steps. How much more could you provide for your family and yourself? What new qualities of life could you enjoy? What higher levels of service could you provide your customers?

Why Blockages Occur

Mental, emotional, and spiritual blockages happen because of natural life circumstances, some of which we control, others of which we don't. Whatever the reason for the blocks, we usually accept them as *our reality,* and without challenge acquiesce to them.

Here are some common reasons why our thinking, beliefs, and actions get solidified. It's human nature to:

- Seek security and comfort levels.
- Resist challenges, change, or risk.
- Seek the known and steer clear of the unknown.
- Conform to the influence, opinions, and wishes of other people.
- Focus more on our weaknesses than our strengths.
- Punish ourselves for our mistakes more than rewarding ourselves for our successes.
- Accept life as it comes along, rather than challenging it.

It's normal to avoid the unknown and seek the safety of the known. We often *consciously, and then unconsciously,* accept our current conditions, because not accepting them creates stress. We don't really like stress because we perceive it as negative.

But, stress, or tension, can take two directions. It can cause us to shut down, or it can motivate us to open up and think and act differently.

Without a success orientation, admitting blockages can create discomfort for our self-images. Construed one way, it might imply that we haven't been "good" or "done our best" in the past. But viewed in the context of growth and a desire to become our best, it becomes okay to admit them. In fact, it's exhilarating to think how we can be more, contribute more, and enjoy a higher quality of life when we internally feel worthy of increased rewards.

True professionals are always interested in getting better, and know that "getting better" is an inner emotional and spiritual game, not just the gaining of knowledge.

Needs That Drive Our Acceptance of Blockages

Let me stress that all of us, without challenge, create boundaries to fulfill certain unconscious needs we have. We then have difficulty releasing these needs and we strenuously hold on to them.

These inner needs basically function either to reward or punish us, depending on our individual level of self-esteem. If we don't feel worthy of higher success, we'll demonstrate a powerful, yet unconscious, need to prove this self-assessment by our negative intentions and their resulting self-defeating behaviors. On the other hand, when we do feel worthy of higher success—because of the value we create for people—that inner need will trigger positive, proactive, success-producing behaviors. This causes us to think and act in ways that bring us increased success.

We all have a deep inner need to think, to make decisions, and to act consistently with our unconscious beliefs about how valuable and deserving we are. Our daily sales behaviors act as loyal servants to our inner perceptions and lead us to goals we unconsciously believe we're worthy of achieving. Usually, without questioning it, we accept these perceptions as reality.

It's here that many distortions occur. Not every perception we have of ourselves is accurate, because we often don't understand the truth about ourselves.

What are some of these internal needs that silently control your inner beliefs, which then influence your sales and productivity? Let's think of a few.

- *Your self-esteem.* You have a deep need to perform consistently with your inner beliefs about who you are, what's possible for you to sell, and what you deserve to enjoy in life rewards.

- *Your culture.* You'll generally perform consistently with the success level of people in your culture.
- *Your belief of what normal sales behavior is.* You'll observe the average sales of people around you and assume that this is the norm.
- *Your religious beliefs.* You may have limiting religious beliefs forced upon you, by people whose aim is to control you, that make you feel powerless to oppose limiting forces within your environment.
- *Yielding to the control of others.* You may have people in your life who have a selfish need to control you—to keep you within their boundaries.
- *Your manager's belief in you.* This will influence how you sell or operate.
- *Your organization's values.* These values, implied or voiced, will influence you as they align or conflict with yours.

As you think about these influences, what do you discover? Do you uncover any conflict? How do they possibly influence what you think you should be selling or earning?

When you begin to discover certain inner needs that create blockages to your productivity, the question becomes "How do I deal with them?" Do you attack them head-on, or is there a more effective way?

Now let's examine the following principles of human action.

Emotions Are More Powerful Than Willpower

Moving past blockages isn't an issue of your willpower. You can't mentally muscle your way through them. In fact, the more willpower, effort, or tenacity you exhibit in overcoming them, the more they are usually strengthened. You can't change emotions by conscious effort.

> Your inner feelings and beliefs are much more
> powerful than your willpower.

Take the common enemy of salespeople, call reluctance, which is generally a fear of rejection or failure. A deeper and more subtle emotion is our fear of success. Yes, fear of success. Many of us unconsciously dread higher successes because they will probably take us out of our comfort zone. This creates an inner resistance, because to change, or become more successful, would necessitate giving up the old hallowed thoughts, beliefs, the emotional or even spiritual dogmas to which we might have a strong need to hang on.

Often the more we try to change our behaviors—making more calls, seeing higher level decision makers, closing harder—the more we frustrate our performance and shut down emotionally.

Later in this chapter I'll give you a process for moving past limiting beliefs. You'll learn a method that doesn't involve discipline, or slugging it out with natural life resistances, but rather releasing yourself from the need to hold on to old, limiting influences or perceptions.

Let's think more about these blockages.

Most Blockages Are in Our Minds

Chances are, whatever is currently causing a blockage in your life is self-perceived. You're unconsciously saying, "I can't sell more because . . ." Your restricted vision is only allowing you to see life within the boundaries that you yourself have built.

Relax because this happens to all of us. Emerson wrote, "Everything is impossible until we see a success." So our further sales growth is literally impossible until we "see" ourselves succeeding outside the walls that have previously contained us.

Inner Boundaries

Our "I Think" doesn't always reveal the "truth" to us. It can play games with us to keep our focus on the constraints.

A friend whom I knew for years had a very high desire to succeed in selling. His achievement drive was much higher than his level of success indicated. He had grown up in a family with low income and living standards. Growing up, he dreamed of living in a home in a nice neighborhood, driving a new automobile, and educating his children in excellent schools. He wanted things for his family that he had never had growing up.

He worked his way through college and got a job selling that took him out of town a lot. His new wife resented his travel, and both she and her mother began to let him know of their displeasure. He enjoyed excellent sales results for his first few months, but as pressure from the home front increased, his sales began to sputter.

As the gap between his desired sales performance and his actual sales results widened, he began to suffer extreme stress. Because of his inner drive he worked harder, but to no avail. It seemed that the more he tried the more sluggish his sales became, and the more stressed out he became.

He bought several sales books, thinking that his problem was a lack of knowledge about sales skills. He went to a speaker's rally, where he heard speakers tell the audience of salespeople how easy selling was, that all you had to do to be successful was to learn and practice some "effective closes."

He tried these, and things got bleaker. His self-esteem plummeted. His marriage was on the rocks, and the exciting anticipation of a nice home for his family, of a good education for his future kids—all vanished into depression, self-blame, and hopelessness.

After months of this negative conflict, he was released from his sales

Common Roadblocks for Salespeople

Here are some common roadblocks that keep salespeople imprisoned in limited production levels.

- Limited view of what selling is
- Inadequate belief in their own abilities to do what they think selling is
- Negative support systems
- Poverty consciousness that doesn't allow them to see their true possibilities
- Old, outdated, accumulated beliefs that were held by their parents
- Locked into an environment that doesn't allow higher success.
- Inability to erase memories of old failures or defeats
- Conflicts between the selling activities they're asked to do and their inner values
- Unwillingness to take personal responsibility for their own success
- Deep sense of unworthiness

It isn't easy to discover the real inner needs that create our blocks. Because we have blocks, we can't see beyond them: if we could see past them, they wouldn't be blocks. So they're not going to jump out at you; you have to do some searching.

job and took a routine, forty-hour-a-week job in an assembly plant—all to satisfy his wife and her mother, so they could have more "home life."

He then resigned himself to the "truth" that he wasn't cut out for selling, wasn't really good at it, and beside all that, his "fantasies," as his wife referred to his goals, weren't possible after all.

He went through the next few years explaining to people that he "just wasn't cut out to be a salesman."

What a tragedy.

A rare experience? Not at all.

Remember These Interactions

Blockages are effects that happen due to certain causes.

Remember the model below?

What's happening is that the choices or decisions we make in our "I Think" are constantly interacting with the beliefs, values, and "spirit of truth" in our "I Am," triggering certain emotions that then go on to influence our external behaviors.

The chart on page 66 takes you through some different interactions that trigger emotions and lead to predictable behaviors.

Behaviors

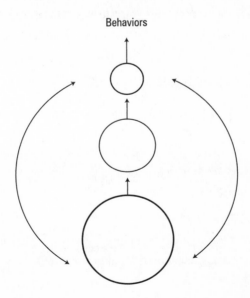

Cause & Effect Interactions

Choice In "I Think"	Beliefs in "I Am"	Triggered Emotions	Resulting Behaviors
To create high value for clients	"That's the right thing to do."	Confidence, Energy, Pride	High calling level
To tell a half-truth to get by	"That's not correct."	Remorse, Guilt, Fear of future contact	Avoidance
To sell only what we believe in	"I need to be honest and truthful."	Confidence, Feel good about self.	Frequent follow-ups, Good client contact
"Selling is doing something *to* people for *my* benefit."	"This doesn't feel right on the inside, but I need to make a sale."	Self-loathing, Don't feel good about actions	Shuts down, Calls at lower levels, Transaction-focused

As you understand this process you can often trace back behaviors to the causes that produced them. You can then see that the emotions were triggered by the conflict or congruence between your conscious choices and your unconscious beliefs or values. Admittedly, this self-analysis isn't always easy, or comfortable; but it does help us better understand our behaviors. The following questions can help you extract answers.

Questions to Ask Yourself

In a sense you must know where you are now before you can define where you want to be, or else you won't understand the required distance you have to travel. To expand your area-of-the-possible, it helps to understand where the starting point is.

Here are some questions that may help you.

1. How do you define selling?
2. How do you view your actual ability to sell on higher levels?
3. What are you being asked to do that is congruent, or in conflict with, your basic values?

4. What sales activities do you enjoy doing? Why?

5. What sales activities do you not enjoy doing? Why not?

6. How do you feel about the value that you, your product, or your service gives to customers above what they pay you for it?

7. When someone asks you what you do, what do you tell them? What thoughts or emotions go through you when you tell them?

8. When you get up in the morning and face the day, how do you feel about it?

9. Who in your life has a selfish need to control you?

10. Who in your life encourages you?

11. Who in your life discourages you?

12. With whom can you share your deepest, honest feelings or thoughts without censorship, rejection, or judgment?

13. Who in your life gives you unconditional acceptance and support?

14. How does your spouse, partner, closest friend, or family describe what you do to others?

15. Who tells you that you should be doing something different than selling?

16. What are your deepest spiritual values?

17. How do these spiritual values match your role as a salesperson?

18. What environmental influences are affecting your job?

19. Which of your company's values are either congruent with or in conflict with yours?

20. What did your parents tell you about your ability to succeed as you were growing up?

21. What did you learn from your parents about money?

22. How does the way you handle your money cause you to feel secure, or insecure?

23. How do you feel about purchasing a home that's three times the price of your current home's value?

24. Whom might you move away from if you were to earn three times what you're currently earning?

25. To what extent are you able to allow people to compliment you or do nice things for you when you deserve it?

26. Who in your life do you most want to please? What do you do to please them? When you please them, how do you feel about it?

27. How would your customers describe to others what you make happen for them?
28. Who in your life would be jealous or resent your becoming more successful?
29. Who attempts to dump guilt on you?
30. What is the level of sales that you'd consider to be impossible for you to sell at?

Now go back and read these questions again and mentally answer each one. Check off three or four that might be creating conflict for you. Then get a pad of paper and a pen, reflect on these three or four questions, and write down the first thoughts that jump into your mind.

Set aside some time this week, get in a quiet place where you'll not be distracted or interrupted, and go through this process. If after reading and thinking about the question, no answers or thoughts come, go to the next one. Write any thoughts that pop into your mind, no matter how good or bad, right or wrong, healthy or unhealthy, moral or immoral. Just write.

When you finish the exercise, quickly read your responses, absorb what you've written, and then tear up the pages and dispose of them.

As you do this, you'll discover that stuff begins to surface that you've kept bottled up. Much of this reveals "truths" about yourself that you've kept well hidden from your consciousness. Some of it may shock your moral or logical senses, but better out than kept in.

It will help you shed your need to be perfect.

Working Through Your Blockages

It's time to stop and seriously define three or four blockages that may be restricting your future growth and success. The following steps will help you.

STEP 1: Define and write out a statement that answers these questions:

- "What people, places, things, or circumstances are influencing the *who* I perceive myself to be?"
- "What level of sales success is possible for me, and what level is impossible for me? What is the dividing line between these two?"

- "What life rewards are possible for me to enjoy? What are not possible? What is the dividing line between these two?"

Your answers to these preceding questions might be something like:

- "My old friends don't share my desire to improve my life and achieve more."
- "Probably $600,000 per year sales is about the most I could ever sell in my market."
- "Funding my children's education and taking the family on annual vacations may not both be possible."

The next question isn't easy, because the real reason has been buried deep within your "I Am." But let's give it a go; start with your best response. This shouldn't be a one-time activity you do, but rather an ongoing one. The truth is that growth is in continually doing this process, discovering and moving past mental, emotional, and spiritual blocks for your lifetime. Since you'll never reach true perfection in this life, there'll always be blocks.

STEP 2: Ask, "What causes me to set these boundaries?"
This question might suggest some answers like:

- "My old friends' achievement drive is lower than mine."
- "$600,000 per year is the most I've ever sold."
- "I'm not sure I can earn enough to contribute to our children's education fund, and take the kind of family vacation we've dreamed about."

STEP 3: Ask, "Why am I allowing these influences to become my beliefs?"
Here are some examples.

- "Why do I allow my old friends' low achievement drive to influence me?" Your answer might be, "Because I feel comfortable with them and don't want them to think I think I'm better than they are."
- "Why do I think $600,000 per year sales is my limit?" Your

answer might be, "Because Mary Johnson sells $800,000 per year, and I could never sell as much as she does."

- "Why do I feel that I can't earn enough to contribute to our children's education fund and take the kind of vacation we've dreamed of?" Your answer might be, "Because I've never earned that much before."

STEP 4: Define the old perceptions you've held that caused you to have these feelings.

They might sound something like these:

- "I should be loyal to my old friends, and not do anything that causes them to feel that I think I'm better than they are."
- "I don't really want to challenge Mary Johnson because I'd probably lose."
- "We never took nice vacations when I grew up and I feel a bit extravagant even planning them."

Whatever comes into your mind as you ask what's causing you to set old boundaries, write them down. Don't strive to sound good. No one's going to see your responses. Again, if nothing jumps into your mind, just move on. As you continue this exercise, over and over, eventually answers will be transmitted to your "I Think" from the inner recordings in your "I Am."

STEP 5: Identify why you need to hang on to these old perceptions.

You have a strong inner need to hang on to your old perceptions and their resulting behaviors and life manifestations. There's something that's keeping you from letting go of them. It may be your resistance to change, or being more successful might actually conflict with your religious beliefs or the beliefs of influential people around you. Or the reason could go much deeper.

Most of the time it's our own self-images that won't allow us to perform on different levels. Here are some "reasons" I've heard from salespeople.

- "My wife (or husband) dislikes the insecurity of my job, and I can't change that."

- "It's a sin to focus on making money."
- "I'm afraid that my parents and siblings will feel that I'm socially and economically distancing myself from them."
- "No one in my family has ever done well in selling."
- "I don't like to be labeled a 'salesman.'"

The needs we unconsciously hang on to can go much deeper than I've just indicated. They can be expressed like this.

- "I can't admit that I could be doing better, because it would indicate that I haven't been doing my best in the past, and I've always been very conscientious."
- "I'm reluctant to set higher goals, because I don't want to try and then fail."
- "I'm just not worthy of higher success."
- "I feel stuck in this job, city, relationship, and I don't know how to get out."
- "I didn't get a college degree just to end up selling."

The real needs for hanging on to old perceptions are at the control panel in our inner motivation. They'll continue there until we dig them out, disarm them, and/or move past them. They mostly stem from a deep feeling of unworthiness.

STEP 6: Release your need to hold on to old limiting perceptions.
Here I'm going to ask you to depart from much of what you've been conditioned to believe about personal growth. In our success-oriented, modern culture, we've been taught the virtues of *discipline, trying harder, effort, attack-the-problem,* and *do-it-now, action-is-the-thing* thinking.

It's not that they don't have a place in the positive actions we take, but in dealing with emotions they can actually be destructive to our personal growth. In some situations they can even serve to solidify our boundaries and strengthen our self-imposed limitations and blockages.

Self-discipline is necessary to carry out activities and other self-management skills, but it can have a reverse effect if we're attempting to change old self-perceptions. For instance, the more you strain and strive not to worry, the more you actually elicit this negative emotion. The more you try to go to sleep, the more awake you become. The more you try to relax, the more tense you get. The more you strive to feel an emotion, the more you drive it away.

The secret to many of life's challenges is simply, *Let go!* Quit striving. Relax. Chill out. Cool it. Instead of trying to change a belief or perception, simply accept it as how you felt at a certain time in the past. Then begin the process of releasing the need to continue to feel, believe, or think the way you once did.

Here's a process for doing it.

Releasing Outdated Perceptions

1. Accept the old perception as what you believed to be true in the past. Say to yourself, "I accept this belief as what I thought to be true in the *past.*"

2. Allow yourself to have held this past perception. Say, "I allow myself to have believed it to be true *at that time.*"

3. Separate your past from your today. Say, "I now choose to separate this perception of the *past* from my realities of *today.*"

4. Release yourself from the need to hold on to old perceptions. Say, "I now choose to *let go* of any need to hold on to this old, limiting perception."

5. Repeat this process until your "I Think" sends it to dwell deeply in your "I Am." When you catch yourself experiencing the old perception say, "Stop! Stop!" Then immediately repeat this process.

Allowing This Process to Free You

You can do this process on several levels. Anytime in your waking hours that you have a couple minutes you can mentally go through the process of saying to yourself:

1. "I accept the old belief that I shouldn't live in a more affluent neighborhood as being true in the *past.*"
2. "I allow myself to have believed it to be true *at that time.*"
3. "I now choose to separate this perception of the past from my realities of *today.*"
4. "I now choose to *let go* of any need to hold on to this old, limiting perception."

Of course, just saying it won't immediately make it happen. But when you do it with repetition over a period of weeks, and emotionally internalize the rewards that moving past it will bring you, you'll begin to drill it into the unconscious beliefs in your "I Am."

Then, whenever you catch yourself acting or thinking in ways that reveal the old perception is still guiding you, bring yourself up short and say to yourself, "Stop it!" Then immediately repeat the process. Every time your "logical mind" tells you that you should hang on to the old need, consciously visualize the rewards you'll enjoy when you move into your new goals.

Deeper Programming

There are a couple of ways you can release old perceptions and their causal needs in your "I Am" more quickly. First, memorize the five steps for releasing outdated perceptions, and then while you're in that twilight state just before going to sleep or immediately upon waking, go through the process. You'll have less mental clutter and more of the message can be absorbed in your "I Am."

Within days of doing this consistently, you'll begin to do it unconsciously.

You can also follow the process at the end of relaxation or meditation time. If you meditate, do it when your brain goes into an alpha state—the time when you're awake but have released your body sensations.

Are You Ready To Enjoy Higher Achievement?

Is your achievement drive strong enough to pull you through the changes you must make to move to higher levels of sales? Can you see higher achievement being consistent with who you are?

You'll answer these questions with your actions.

HOW TO GAIN THE MOST FROM THIS CHAPTER

Carl Jung once wrote that "it's only when the conscious mind confronts the unconscious that a provisional reaction will ensue which determines the subsequent procedure."

In our language, it's when our "I Think" confronts our "I Am," and challenges it to give us answers, that hunches, ideas, and insights begin to flow from the wisdom that permeates the deep recesses of our unconscious. This reaction can then automatically influence our outer behaviors.

As we listen to these interactions and are willing to go through the discomfort of sailing into unknown waters, we grow. And grow we must in order to enjoy higher sales productivity.

Continue to mull over these ideas during the week. There's certainly enough here to challenge the serious student of success for a lifetime. But for now write the five steps of the Releasing Outdated Perceptions Process on a sheet of paper or index cards, or enter them in your computer. Learn and memorize the steps. If you get a break during your workday, go through them again. With practice and time you'll begin to uncover new insights.

As you do these steps, you'll discover that your energy, self-confidence, and actual external behaviors will become stronger and stronger.

And forget "trying harder." Don't try to remove blocked thinking with self-discipline alone. The secret is in *accepting* and *releasing* old thinking and their resulting behavior patterns.

Here's a helpful self-suggestion for this week: "I release myself from any emotional need to hang on to old self-defeating beliefs."

A Special Challenge for This Chapter

This chapter can be a "bombshell" experience for you. It has been designed to help you identify and work through old, limiting perceptions, and the needs that drive them. And it will work for any success-oriented person.

Let's stop for a moment and keep a clear focus on where we're going with this. Remember:

1. We have an inner belief boundary that defines who we are, what's possible for us to sell, and what life rewards we deserve to enjoy.
2. This boundary is based on your past perceptions and not on actual fact or truth.
3. We live out these inner beliefs without questioning their authenticity.
4. We have a strong inner need to hold on to these old beliefs and experience difficulty releasing them.
5. Our sales and life circumstances won't usually change until we release the need to hold on to these old beliefs and move past them.

It's important to keep these steps in mind, since it's easy to be "logical" and get mentally lost in the process.

I realize that what I've presented in this chapter requires lots of questioning, reflection, and answering. You'll have to determine whether or not it's worth it to you. I know this can be done in the context of busy days and weeks, because I've done it. It's a matter of deciding to *find the time*.

And as I've done it, it has changed my view of my possibilities, my actual abilities to sell on higher levels, and my belief of what life rewards I deserve to enjoy.

Come back to this chapter when you can. Each time you'll be at a different level of growth, so you'll gain higher benefits each time.

3 SHATTERING BLOCKAGES OF YOUR SUCCESS

Assessment

Please take a few moments and check off the number that best describes your present beliefs, boundaries, or behaviors. Use these descriptors as guidelines.

> 5–Always true, without exception
> 4–Mostly true
> 3–True more often than not
> 2–True only part of the time
> 1–True only occasionally

1. I'm satisfied with the way I am now.	5 4 3 2 1 1 2 3 4 5	1. I'm always seeking ways to improve.
2. I seek the path of least resistance.	5 4 3 2 1 1 2 3 4 5	2. I'm willing to do whatever I have to do to be more effective.
3. I feel trapped in my current condition.	5 4 3 2 1 1 2 3 4 5	3. I have a "no-limitation" belief in my possibilities.
4. I dwell a lot on what I don't have.	5 4 3 2 1 1 2 3 4 5	4. I think mostly about reaching higher goals.
5. I tend to yield to other people's opinions of me.	5 4 3 2 1 1 2 3 4 5	5. I tend to hold fast to my own self-beliefs when I'm right.
6. I feel that my sales opportunities are limited.	5 4 3 2 1 1 2 3 4 5	6. I actively seek new ways to sell on higher levels.
7. I often give in to my fears and this influences my sales behaviors.	5 4 3 2 1 1 2 3 4 5	7. I'm aware of my negative emotions, and don't allow them to rule my behaviors.
8. I view selling as getting people to do what I want them to do.	5 4 3 2 1 1 2 3 4 5	8. I view selling as helping people and creating value for them.
9. My sales are mostly controlled by factors that I can't influence.	5 4 3 2 1 1 2 3 4 5	9. My sales are mostly controlled by my own beliefs, expectations, and behaviors.
10. I can't release myself from mistakes of the past.	5 4 3 2 1 1 2 3 4 5	10. I'm able to put my past behind me and view the future in positive ways.

- Add up the numbers in the right-hand column. _____
- Add up the numbers in the left-hand column. _____
- Subtract the left-hand column total from the right-hand column total and score yourself. _____

Assessments scoring guide is on page 35.

Keeping Score—Chapter 3

Behavior that gets evaluated, gets improved.

On a scale of 1–10, please evaluate your performance of each of these parts of the Breakthrough Process.

	S	M	T	W	T	F	S
1. I became aware of my current behaviors.							
2. I noticed the attitudes or feelings that influenced these behaviors.							
3. I attempted to connect these feelings and behaviors with the unconscious beliefs that might be driving them.							
4. I selected new beliefs that I'd like to have embedded in my "I Am."							
5. I had the courage to go through change, conflict, and ambiguity.							
Total Each Day							

4 Achievement

Understanding the Four Core Success Factors

THERE ARE FOUR CORE TRAITS THAT HIGHLY SUCCESSFUL salespeople all share. Regardless of what you sell, these four traits are in the marrow that sustains your high achievement. People who possess them always do better on their jobs and with other people. These four traits are the cause; high success is the effect.

Here they are:

1. Strong goal clarity
2. High achievement drive
3. Healthy emotional intelligence
4. Excellent social skills

But hearing what they are doesn't mean you have them, any more than knowing about pole vaulting will help you vault nineteen feet or reading a book on flying will prepare you to pilot an airplane.

By the time you finish this chapter, you'll know and understand these core traits, but that's only the beginning. You can spend your lifetime *developing* them on deeper levels, and the result will be greater enrichment and success.

Strong Goal Clarity

Goal clarity is having clear, specific, written descriptions of what you want to happen in your future. Your goals don't necessarily have to be save-the-planet size objectives. They may be, but more likely they're things like the following:

- Reach a specific sales target
- Acquire a new home or enjoy an improvement in your current one
- Earn a certain amount of money or job success
- Earn a degree
- Develop a new habit or skill
- Own a new car
- Achieve permanent slimness or enjoy a healthier lifestyle
- Enjoy a family vacation
- Develop a comprehensive financial plan
- Develop a specific spiritual or emotional quality

The problem is that very few people have goal clarity. All those entering our Integrity Systems development courses are asked to assess themselves in twelve different dimensions. Almost without fail, they rate themselves lowest in *goal clarity.*

If you agree that having goal clarity is the beginning of most successful accomplishments, you'll find this low self-scoring to be startling. It's like losing a race before even getting out of the starting block, because we don't know where the finish line is.

Regardless of what your goals are—whether they're career-oriented, family-focused, financial, spiritual, going fishing, a trip to New Zealand, whatever—it begins with a clear focus of:

1. *Where* you want to go
2. *When* you want to arrive
3. *How* you're going to get there

Let me admit that I don't always practice what I preach. In fact, I often catch myself going through and intellectualizing all this, only to discover that while I know how to set goals—I teach it and help others do it—I haven't actually experienced it for a while.

My knowing often blocks my doing.

Assess Yourself

The following is a goal clarity self-assessment. Take a few moments and score yourself in the ten subsets.

Goal Clarity Assessment

Please take a moment and score yourself from 1–10 on each of the following statements. One means the statement is *never* descriptive, and ten means it's *always* descriptive of your behaviors.

1. I write down clear personal and work-related goals that guide my sales achievement.

   1   2   3   4   5   6   7   8   9   10

2. I take time daily to picture my goals clearly in my mind's eye.

   1   2   3   4   5   6   7   8   9   10

3. I write down specific measurements and strategies to help me reach goals.

   1   2   3   4   5   6   7   8   9   10

4. I use positive thoughts and images to expand my beliefs about my ability to attain high goals.

   1   2   3   4   5   6   7   8   9   10

5. I constantly learn new skills that build the strengths I need to achieve my goals.

   1   2   3   4   5   6   7   8   9   10

6. I constantly review and revise my goals as I work to achieve them.

   1   2   3   4   5   6   7   8   9   10

7. I break my goals down into small steps that I can work on daily.

   1   2   3   4   5   6   7   8   9   10

8. When I set a new goal, I set a specific time to achieve it.

   1   2   3   4   5   6   7   8   9   10

9. I internally believe my goals to be within my possibilities.

   1   2   3   4   5   6   7   8   9   10

10. When I set goals, I mentally focus on the end-result benefits rather than on the difficulties of achieving them.

    1   2   3   4   5   6   7   8   9   10

Total Score _____

Study these ten statements and you'll have a very good overall understanding of what goal clarity is all about.

Inner Needs Drive Goal Achievement

In most goal achievement discussions the question comes up, "What goals are possible for me, and which ones aren't?" As I've mentioned, any goal is possible if someone with your general abilities, training, resources, and desire level has achieved a similar one. This fact can help you form a new view of your own possibilities.

But let's look at it a different way: your *inner needs* always drive your goal possibilities. Whatever need level you're on will determine the size goals you set and reach, and the size you don't think you can reach.

When you understand "need levels" you'll know one of the deepest mysteries of goal achievement. Need levels are stages or situations that our life experiences place us in. They can be imposed by economic, emotional, spiritual, environmental, or relationship circumstances.

To help you understand this in relation to yourself I've designed a Progression of Human Needs model. Please look it over and consider the different levels:

Understanding the Model

Here are the points that will help you understand what's motivating you, as well as what new goals will be realistic or unrealistic for you.

1. You're motivated by needs, wants, and values—for hope of gain and relief of pain.
2. Whatever need level you're on, you're primarily concerned with satisfying that specific one and are blinded to others.
3. You can be on different need levels in different places of your life; areas with the lowest need levels will usually demand greater attention.
4. When a need level is satisfied, you'll automatically move to the next higher one.
5. Your goals will be unconsciously screened out unless they address your present need level.
6. Your goals should be focused on the need level that will both satisfy your current level and move you to the next higher one.

Progression of Human Needs

Survival	Security	Knowledge	Self-Esteem	Self-Expression	Wisdom	Transcendence
• To preserve life – Physically – Emotionally – Financially	• To feel safe • To experience freedom • To control choices • To determine own direction	• To know how to function in life situations • To know how to answer questions, solve problems, and make decisions • To make positive choices • To satisfy curiosity	• To give and receive love • To feel good about one's self • To experience satisfying relationships • To forgive and feel forgiven	• To achieve • To express uniqueness • To move toward purpose • To enjoy	• To understand how and why things are • To discern • To relate cause and effect • To know that you know	• To transcend humanness • To move beyond material values • To seek a higher state • To know true peace

Where you are in each of these seven dimensions influences your sales. Your ability to sell on higher levels isn't divorced from the other parts of your life. Unfortunately, a high percentage of people stay in the first three levels.

Consider, for example, a person who's just experienced the death of a loved one, a devastating bankruptcy, or the loss of a job. It's possible that he or she would quickly move to a lower level of survival or security, either emotionally, financially, or professionally. This person probably wouldn't be indulging in esoteric or intellectual advancement thoughts; rather, he'd be concerned about solving his current situation. He would want to move past the pain of loss, deal with the problems of a bankruptcy, or find another job. His goals should be to move to a higher level. Goals to go beyond the next level would probably have little motivational pull.

To help you apply this to your own situation, the following self-assessment permits you to graphically plot where you are in five different areas of your life.

Plotting Your Need Levels

Look at each category and put a check mark in the appropriate column, from 1, Survival, to 7, Transcendence, or the highest level.

	1	2	3	4	5	6	7
1. Financial							
2. Social							
3. Family							
4. Career							
5. Spiritual							
6. Personal Health							

Remember, the area of lowest need will usually demand the most attention, and will continue its silent pleadings until its needs are met. Attempting to reach higher goals in other areas of your life will meet unconscious resistance until these basic needs have been met.

Achievement Drive

Achievement drive is energy. This energy is released from within you when you have goal clarity. The amount of energy you release is first determined by your level of desire for the goal, to what extent you internally believe it's possible to attain, and how worthy you feel to enjoy the goal. These factors then influence the effort, commitment, and persistence you'll exhibit in the pursuit of your goals.

The late David McClelland, who for more than fifty years researched this power at Harvard University, theorized that people with high rankings in achievement drive begin with a high internal need for it.

It's also important to understand that achievement drive acts as a multiplying factor. It actually *multiplies* the sum of all the talents, skills, resources, and assets of individuals, organizations, and nations.

Please look at the following model and, just for the fun of it, on a scale of 1–10, rate yourself in each area:

	Product Knowledge	_____
+	Sales Skills	_____
+	Inherent Abilities	_____
+	Selling Experience	_____
+	Products and Resources	_____
×	Achievement Drive	_____
=	Sales Power	_____

This helps you rate your success power. As you increase your achievement drive, you'll automatically multiply your total effectiveness.

Where Does Achievement Drive Originate?

The path to understanding where this energy originates is strewn with many paradoxes and anomalies. For example, consider two siblings. One child becomes a highly successful surgeon, and the other ends up a penniless alcoholic. Both are from the same family and home environment. So what creates the difference? It's usually a combination of factors.

In an attempt to bring some degree of understanding to the cause of achievement drive, let me list several common ones:

1. Emphasis on achievement in families as children grew up
2. Feelings of inadequacy or low self-esteem in early childhood
3. Teachers or mentors who talked about achievement and the ability to reach whatever goals one wanted
4. Traditional family or religious values
5. Birth order among siblings
6. Environmental influences
7. Physical size and rate of maturity (especially in men)
8. Education
9. Encouraging relationships
10. Entrepreneurial personal traits

Of course, there are other influences on achievement drive, but these are some of the most common and complex ones.

I've noticed that the same dynamics cause high achievement drive in some people and low drive in others, so it's obvious that other factors come into play. But what are they and how do they converge? As you read and understand more of the life factors that influence each person's "I Am" dimension, you'll have more of your questions answered. You'll understand more about your entrepreneurial tendencies—a willingness to take risks, the valuing of opportunity over security, indulgence of your restless mind, or a propensity to dream. These and other personal traits become the catalysts that propel people in paradoxical ways.

But let's get back to you. Please look at the following profile. Read each statement and score yourself.

Achievement Drive Self-Assessment

Please take time to fill in the following Achievement Drive Self-Assessment. It's a quick one-minute way to take a look at yourself.

1. People refer to me as being "highly motivated."

       1   2   3   4   5   6   7   8   9   10

2. I'm much more goal-oriented than process-oriented.

       1   2   3   4   5   6   7   8   9   10

3. I have a very high amount of inner drive to achieve sales success.

       1   2   3   4   5   6   7   8   9   10

4. I am constantly reading self-help books and listening to high achievers.

       1   2   3   4   5   6   7   8   9   10

5. I'm always picking the brains of successful people.

       1   2   3   4   5   6   7   8   9   10

6. I'm emotionally charged with a "high" whenever I accomplish a success-ful goal.

       1   2   3   4   5   6   7   8   9   10

7. My need for achievement overpowers my fear of rejection.

       1   2   3   4   5   6   7   8   9   10

8. I am willing to take calculated risks; in fact, I thrive on them.

       1   2   3   4   5   6   7   8   9   10

9. I'm always looking for new ways and ideas to reach higher goals.

       1   2   3   4   5   6   7   8   9   10

10. I often fantasize about the rewards that reaching my goals will bring me.

       1   2   3   4   5   6   7   8   9   10

Total Score _____

People with high achievement drive think differently than others. They think about reaching goals, the rewards that reaching goals will bring them, and the fulfillment they'll enjoy. They fantasize about achievement. They usually talk about goal attainment with others. They go places, read things, and do activities that high achievers do.

High achievers think in terms of the *rewards* for reaching sales goals, not just the reaching of sales goals. They're motivated to serve cus-tomers exceptionally well, earn high respect, enjoy a certain lifestyle, and other benefits.

Again, all this works consistently with your current need level. Your rewards should be something you'd enjoy when you're on the next high-est need level.

How Is the Level of Achievement Drive Influencing Your Life?

Your level of achievement drive is housed in your "I Am" and influences your career choices, friends, compensation, where you live, where your kids go to school, who you vote for, what your expectations are, how you package yourself, and your views of your own possibilities. This core influence has its thumb prints on most of your life circumstances.

Occasionally in my seminars, a hand goes up and someone says, "Isn't this all pretty neurotic? Isn't this a pretty unbalanced life you're talking about?" My answer is, "Of course, it could be! It all depends on balance and values."

Some of the most unhappy and emotionally unhealthy people on earth are multizillionaires who have totally given their lives over to making money or building organizations. They may not know their children, may have been through a half dozen unsuccessful relationships, and stepped on many people.

That's not the kind of life I'm writing about. I'm talking about balance, which happens from living a values-centered life. This, of course, begins with a goal, a choice you make that's values-driven.

How Do I Increase My Desire for Higher Goals?

In his research, McClelland discovered that one common factor kept recurring in people who demonstrated high achievement drive. They all fantasized about achievement more than people whom he studied who had low drives.

This eventually led him to ask the obvious question: Can achievement drive be increased within individuals by simply increasing the frequency of people's fantasizing about it? The results of his subsequent experimentation exceeded his expectations. He concluded that what people daydream about ultimately influences their actions and goals. About this time R. W. Burris of the University of Indiana completed a similar study with students and concluded the same thing: attempts to alter the thoughts of students influenced their achievement drive.

In one experiment, he formed three groups:

1. One group attended eight counseling sessions where both their goals and the use they intended to make of their education were dis-

cussed. Along with this the importance of achievement drive was presented in a way that got students thinking in terms of end results, goals, and achievement.

2. Another group received counseling on how to study but with no reference to achievement drive.

3. A third group received no counseling at all.

At the conclusion of the experiment, all the students were tested again to see if there had been any increase in their need for achievement. Working closely with Burris, McClelland reported, "As predicted . . . the subjects whose achievement motivation had been openly and intensively discussed showed a significant rise in their need for achievement scores."

They found evidence that the scores were real because the students in the first group showed significant increases in their grades. Like the students in these examples, you can begin increasing your achievement drive by fantasizing about goals and the payoff or rewards of reaching them.

You can also meet with a few other people who are highly motivated to reach higher goals and spend time talking about achievement. A continued association with these people can have powerful effects in increasing your own drive.

Keep asking yourself, "What can happen in my future that excites me just thinking about it?" Spend time daydreaming about it. For these moments, suspend logical or rational thought. Feed reward thoughts to your mind.

People who achieve higher goals almost always, consciously or unconsciously, take time for creative fantasy.

What Is Emotional Intelligence?

Basically, emotional intelligence is the ability to:

1. Understand our feelings or emotions and how they influence our external behaviors.

2. Take control of our emotions and do the difficult things that we may not want to do, but must do, in order to achieve our worthwhile goals.

Emotional intelligence is a critical factor in successful performance. This trait is composed of the following activities:

1. Monitoring and understanding your own feelings and emotions and their impact upon your external behaviors
2. Persistently doing result-producing activities despite disappointments, roadblocks, and setbacks
3. Dealing with frustrating and difficult people with patience and even tempered responses
4. Internally motivating yourself without the need for external motivation

Daniel Goleman, writing in his excellent work *Emotional Intelligence,* makes the point, "What makes the difference between stars and the others is not their academic IQ but their *emotional* EQ."

There are two other names for emotional intelligence—*maturity* and *stability.* These can be demonstrated when you respond to life with the following behaviors:

1. Devotion to the truth
2. Acceptance of responsibility for your own actions, commitments, and goals
3. Delaying of gratification
4. Commitment to problem solving

Rather than practicing these disciplines, many people opt to take the easy way out of difficult situations.

A Highly Prized Trait

There's probably not a sales organization in the world that wouldn't like to have more people who exhibit emotional balance in their daily activities. My experience with our client organizations is that there's never enough people with high emotional intelligence to fill sales jobs.

Pause for a moment, and reflect on what we've discussed about emotional intelligence. Consider these questions:

1. What percent of the salespeople that I know or work with would I rate high in this trait?

2. How is this trait not practiced by the people with whom I have contact?

3. What would happen to salespeople's individual confidence and to organizations' overall sales if this trait were more widely practiced by their people?

To avoid possible pain, to duck responsibility and commitment, many people tend to take the easy way out. Yes, we do all kinds of behaviors to avoid possible pain. Ego pain. Relationship pain. The pain of possible failure. The pain of fear of the unknown. The pain of possible customer rejection.

When salespeople face possible rejection, failure, disgrace, self-esteem, or ego damage, it's easy to play weak emotional games. Call reluctance, fear of rejection, ducking responsibility. Taking the easy way out. Being unwilling to hang tough when difficult problems present themselves.

These are manifestations of weaknesses in emotional intelligence. The antidote is courage—calling where we're afraid to call, seeing people we're afraid to see, asking when we're afraid to ask.

But what drives behaviors of avoidance? What drives acts of courage? Why do some people take control of their lives, and others don't?

Values Become the Determinant

In most or all of these situations, it's your internal values that determine which course of action you'll take when coming up against difficult situations.

The subject of values will be touched upon many times in this book, because they form the very core or essence of your "I Am." Your values define who you are more than anything else. They are very accurate predictors of your future success. Strong, positive values open the door to higher success.

With these thoughts in mind, take a look at the next assessment.

Emotional Intelligence
Self-Assessment

Please review the following questionnaire. Rank from 1–10 how descriptive each statement is of your actual behaviors, thoughts, or attitudes.

1. I understand my emotions and how they can influence my sales success.

   1   2   3   4   5   6   7   8   9   10

2. I'm able to maintain an even emotional tone in all selling situations.

   1   2   3   4   5   6   7   8   9   10

3. I'm able to use defeats and rejection as growth steps.

   1   2   3   4   5   6   7   8   9   10

4. My self-esteem is strong enough that I don't lash out at people who criticize or oppose me.

   1   2   3   4   5   6   7   8   9   10

5. I am able to delay gratification and to wait for the right moment to enjoy rewards.

   1   2   3   4   5   6   7   8   9   10

6. I am able to control my emotions and respond positively to rejection or criticism.

   1   2   3   4   5   6   7   8   9   10

7. I am able to monitor my emotions and to clearly understand their impact on my sales activities.

   1   2   3   4   5   6   7   8   9   10

8. Discouragement never alters my path to goal achievement.

   1   2   3   4   5   6   7   8   9   10

9. I seek the truth no matter how easy it would be not to do it.

   1   2   3   4   5   6   7   8   9   10

10. When I take responsibility for a task or commitment, I see it through no matter how difficult it is.

   1   2   3   4   5   6   7   8   9   10

Total Score _____

As you evaluate yourself in these ten areas, you may want to select one or two specific ones to focus and work on. Developing the emotional tensile strength to keep going despite emotional downs isn't always easy. The rewards, though, and the increase in self-esteem can be a strong, cleansing, sweet experience.

Excellent Social Skills

The fourth trait that we have seen in highly successful people is excellent social skills. These interpersonal skills enable you to listen, understand, and respond appropriately to different styles of people and in different settings. They help you adapt to other people's unique pace, tone, and attitudes. To have empathy with them. To crawl into their emotional feelings, understand them, and communicate that understanding. To feel like they feel. To see the world through their eyes.

Excellent social skills run much deeper than "gift of gab," surface-level communication, or cocktail party chatter. They involve the following values, attitudes, and behaviors:

1. Valuing people
2. Listening to what people say and how they feel
3. Understanding what people say and how they feel
4. Responding appropriately to varied social situations
5. Causing others to feel understood

As with the other three traits of highly successful people, here is a social skills self-assessment for you to answer and score for yourself.

Social Skills
Self-Assessment

Please score yourself from 1–10 as to how descriptive each statement is of your actual behaviors.

1. I completely listen to people without interrupting them.

       1   2   3   4   5   6   7   8   9   10

2. I can pick up and understand unspoken meanings from people.

       1   2   3   4   5   6   7   8   9   10

3. I take time to understand people's ideas and concerns before responding to them.

          1   2   3   4   5   6   7   8   9   10

4. When I meet people, my thoughts and behaviors are focused on understanding them rather than on myself.

          1   2   3   4   5   6   7   8   9   10

5. When approaching customers, I always get them talking and me listening as soon as I can.

          1   2   3   4   5   6   7   8   9   10

6. I am able to read body language and pick up on unspoken gestures.

          1   2   3   4   5   6   7   8   9   10

7. I always allow a person's unique behavior to determine how I communicate with them.

          1   2   3   4   5   6   7   8   9   10

8. I can intuitively get people talking about subjects that interest them.

          1   2   3   4   5   6   7   8   9   10

9. People quickly get the message that I am sincere and honest with them.

          1   2   3   4   5   6   7   8   9   10

10. I always remember that each person is silently screaming, "Understand me and make me feel important."

          1   2   3   4   5   6   7   8   9   10

Total Score _____

The Importance of Social Skills

In today's technology-oriented culture, a salesperson's ability to relate to other people still reigns supreme in successful sales job performance. Situations are legion where people who are highly competent technically fail at their sales jobs because they can't get along with people.

Since it's more of a sales skills book, you'll find great help with behavior styles in my book, *Integrity Selling for the 21st Century.* I think you'll find it especially helpful for what it presents about developing social styles. Since people have to work with people, good social skills will always be important for success.

Where Do These Four Traits Reside?

I mentioned earlier that these traits aren't intellectually learned but are experientially developed. They're external behaviors that are driven by your internal values or beliefs in your "I Am."

Let's look again at the three-dimensional model below.

As you review the model, you'll see that it's with your conscious "I Think" that you make decisions, choose to act, set goals, or exercise discipline. When these are undergirded by appropriate values and beliefs in your "I Am", then you're in congruence and you experience positive emotions in your "I Feel."

The Cause and Effect of Having the Four Traits

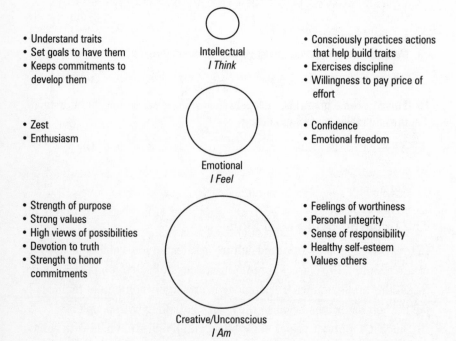

• Understand traits
• Set goals to have them
• Keeps commitments to
  develop them

Intellectual
I Think

• Consciously practices actions
  that help build traits
• Exercises discipline
• Willingness to pay price of
  effort

• Zest
• Enthusiasm

Emotional
I Feel

• Confidence
• Emotional freedom

• Strength of purpose
• Strong values
• High views of possibilities
• Devotion to truth
• Strength to honor
  commitments

Creative/Unconscious
I Am

• Feelings of worthiness
• Personal integrity
• Sense of responsibility
• Healthy self-esteem
• Values others

HOW TO GAIN THE MOST FROM THIS CHAPTER

I've presented to you the four core traits that we've observed in high achievers around the world in our development courses.

1. Strong goal clarity
2. High achievement drive
3. Healthy emotional intelligence
4. Excellent social skills

Here's a simple way to take action and begin your development of the four success factors that I've presented.

1. Score yourself on each of the four self-assessments, being honest about how descriptive each one is of your actual behaviors.
2. Select one of the ten statements from each of the four assessments. Write each on an index card, and carry it with you every day this next week.
3. Read the statements several times each day, and say them as self-suggestions, with enough repetition to drive them into your unconscious thoughts.
4. Practice the actions each day with your customers, and in your social, or family life.

These actions guarantee gradual growth in each of the traits. In addition you may want to think of your need levels, and make sure your goals are consistent with them.

1. Evaluate yourself on the Progression of Human Needs model. Discover your need levels in different areas of your life.
2. Select an activity each day that might help satisfy the level you're on and move you to the next degree of success.

Don't let all these suggestions overwhelm you. I list them as different options. Please choose one or two ideas to practice this week in your real-world contact with people. You can come back to this chapter often, and work on these exercises after you've finished this book.

Remember, growth comes in your application, and in small increments, so be patient.

4 UNDERSTANDING THE FOUR CORE SUCCESS FACTORS

Assessment

Please take a few moments and check off the number that best describes your true present beliefs, boundaries, or behaviors. Use these descriptors as guidelines.

> 5–Always true, without exception
> 4–Mostly true
> 3–True more often than not
> 2–True only part of the time
> 1–True only occasionally

1. I have no specific goals.	5 4 3 2 1 1 2 3 4 5	1. I have clear sales goals, broken down into weekly goals.
2. My goals are much larger than I've ever produced before.	5 4 3 2 1 1 2 3 4 5	2. My goals are set a bit beyond where I've been producing.
3. I've written down goals, but lost them or rarely look at them.	5 4 3 2 1 1 2 3 4 5	3. I refer to my written goals daily, and allow them to drive my activities.
4. I'm so focused on survival, I can't imagine things being different.	5 4 3 2 1 1 2 3 4 5	4. I'm driven by the rewards of reaching my goals.
5. I'm not sure that selling is the right career for me.	5 4 3 2 1 1 2 3 4 5	5. I have a very high desire to succeed in selling.
6. I find I'm often up one day and down the next.	5 4 3 2 1 1 2 3 4 5	6. I handle my emotions well.
7. I allow other people's moods to influence mine.	5 4 3 2 1 1 2 3 4 5	7. I maintain a level of emotional control despite the moods of others.
8. I just can't connect with some people.	5 4 3 2 1 1 2 3 4 5	8. I gain rapport with customers easily.

9. I often catch myself talking too much on a sales call.	5 4 3 2 1	1 2 3 4 5	9. I carefully listen to customers without interrupting them.
10. I'm not too sensitive to customers' behavior styles.	5 4 3 2 1	1 2 3 4 5	10. I easily read and understand people's body language.

- Add up the numbers in the right-hand column. _____
- Add the numbers in the left-hand column. _____
- Subtract the left-hand column total from the right-hand column total and score yourself. _____

Assessments scoring guide is on page 35.

Keeping Score—Chapter 4

Behavior that gets evaluated, gets improved.

On a scale of 1–10, please evaluate your performance of each of these Action Guides.

	S	M	T	W	T	F	S
1. I reviewed the statements on the four assessments today.							
2. I practiced specific statements in my work today.							
3. I evaluated myself on the Progression of Human Needs model today.							
4. I thought of ways I can grow in the four traits today.							
5. I studied or thought of how a happy, successful person demonstrates the four traits today.							
Total Each Day							

5 **Abundance**

Setting Goals for the Future You

YEARS AGO, AS I WAS STRUGGLING TO GET MY TRAINING and development business going, it came to me clearly one day that my thoughts were mainly focused on financial survival. The difficulties of paying my bills and feeding my family kept me focused on just making ends meet, rather than on higher levels of income.

I eventually realized that I was earning what I unconsciously expected to earn and was unknowingly playing mind games to live out these unconscious expectations. For some illogical reason, I was proving to myself that I wasn't motivated for the money in it.

Why I needed to prove this escapes me now. Old tapes, I suppose. An old poverty consciousness had led me to believe that it was wrong to help other people and get paid for it.

It took time for me to understand that I still had a lot of limiting beliefs I had developed growing up.

The incongruous belief that I should help a lot of people but not be paid well for doing it hit me fully when I received a letter from a woman who had just graduated from one of my courses. At first I thought the letter had been written by two totally different people. She began by sharing with me some of the life-changing experiences she'd enjoyed as a result of the course. She wrote things like, "I could never repay you for what I've gained from the course." Then, as if she'd reverted into a totally different person, she spent two pages criticizing me for charging tuition.

At the time, I was struggling just to pay staff and expenses with the small tuition fees we were charging. The unfairness of her letter made me angry but that in itself was extremely creative: I saw that my attempt to keep tuition low was a manifestation of my own self-value at the time. Today, twenty-five years later, our tuitions are at least ten times more than what this woman paid but I can't remember anyone complaining after they graduated.

Old perceptions die slowly. It took some time to reframe old limiting beliefs into a prosperity consciousness. In time, I developed the belief that I should be well paid—when I helped other people earn more, do better in their jobs, and live happier lives.

When I made this decision years ago, I designed a self-suggestion that I then fed my "I Am" through repetitive statements to myself. My self-suggestion was, "God has created everything in abundance. I only have to reach out and claim that which can be mine!"

Abundance Is All Around Us

In time, and with repeated self-suggestions, I began to believe that unlimited prosperity was available in exchange for creating value for other people. This belief began to change my own viewpoint and thinking. I started looking for abundance in nature, in knowledge, and in spiritual blessings. I thought about the vast solar system, the magnificent energy available to people, plants, and earth to recharge, repair, and rebuild. I wanted to observe and learn from people who had an abundance mentality and were not burdened by the limitations I had developed as a result of my past programming.

I began to sell myself on the fact that I should be paid in proportion to the value I created for others. Believing that I should touch the lives of hundreds of thousands of people, helping them enjoy higher prosperity and personal fulfillment, caused me to emotionally understand why I should be highly compensated.

In time I realized that I needed to allow the people whom I helped to return payment to me consistently with the benefits they enjoyed. Denying them this privilege would not be right for either them or me.

I was to learn later that an abundance mentality was indeed necessary before I could actually achieve the higher goals I'd been then setting but not reaching.

Bear in mind that when I write about prosperity, I'm not thinking just about money, although that's an important part of it. Riches come in many packages—friends, family, respect, contentment, fulfillment, a good reputation, spiritual discernment, and wisdom, to name a few.

But where does it all begin?

Your Beliefs Allow Higher Goals to Happen

Goal achievement will be limited, or at best a struggle, until a sense of abundance permeates your "I Am." Until you deeply believe that any goal you set can be achieved, you'll limit yourself.

The mind-set of abundance not only releases us from the constraints and shackles of self-limiting beliefs, it also works as a magnet, drawing us toward the bright sunshine of limitlessness.

As I've suggested several times and in several ways in this book, whatever limits we develop growing up become the belief boundaries of our todays; our lives then become "play-outs" of these beliefs. So many people look haphazardly at life's circumstances and accept them as they perceive they are, rather than challenging them until they discover what they can become.

As we are able to think in realms of greater abundance, our self-beliefs change. Almost invariably we begin to transcend physical, tangible goals, and move more in the direction of intellectual, emotional, and spiritual ones. On this paradoxical pathway we give our lives to the pursuit of a worthy purpose.

Allowing an Internal Congruence for Higher Goals

The model on page 101 shows what factors must be brought into congruence before goals can come into existence.

The arrows between the five dimensions indicate distance, dissonance, or conflict between them. The degree of a conflict determines how strong the blockage of goal achievement is. For instance, if I set a clear goal that's in conflict with my beliefs about my own possibilities, my values, my deep sense of worthiness, or my support systems, I'll probably unconsciously block myself from reaching it.

Goal Achievement Congruence Model

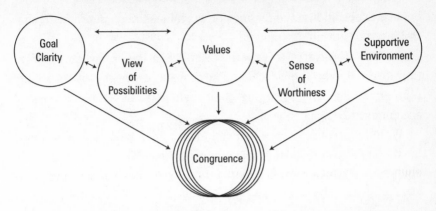

To successfully reach goals you must bring these dimensions into harmony or congruence. This happens experientially, not intellectually. With your "I Think" you choose actions that cause these five dimensions to merge within your "I Am." Most of the Action Guides in this book are designed to help you make this happen.

Your Perceptions Become Your Realities

Not only do your perceptions become your realities, but also your realities and your beliefs are inextricably intertwined. This eternal truth speaks to the very heart of goal achievement.

Herbert Benson writes in *Timeless Healing*, "Our brains cannot distinguish external and internal reality."

He goes on to write, "When you discern that you are being chased, your heart rate increases just as it would if you were really being chased. For your brain, and thus your heart, this is reality."

Writing as a physician, Dr. Benson continues, "Our brains are wired for beliefs and expectancies. When activated, the body can respond as if it would if the belief were a reality, producing deafness or thirst, health or illness."

Benson has spent much of his life exploring the power of people's beliefs since they can influence their physical healing and well being. He and his colleagues use scientific studies with placebo contrasts to prove their points. So whether it's physical or emotional healing, personal success, personal relationships, or some other goal it's clear that your beliefs, expectations, and feelings of worthiness reign supreme in controlling your life circumstances.

Anyone who wants to experience more in life—in whatever form they desire it to be—must understand that success begins by reframing, reprogramming, and enlarging their individual belief boundaries to accommodate expanded goals.

With these concepts as a foundation for understanding, you're ready for the step-by-step Goal Achievement System. This system will help you attain goal clarity, build belief in those goals, develop whatever new strengths you must have, and monitor all this to a successful conclusion—goal achievement.

A Goal Achievement System

The Goal Achievement System has five parts:

1. Setting goals
2. Planning strategy
3. Building belief
4. Developing strengths
5. Managing progress

I've put this into a logical order so that, rather than experiencing goal setting as a hit-or-miss, stab-in-the-dark system, you'll learn a workable process.

The Goal Achievement System

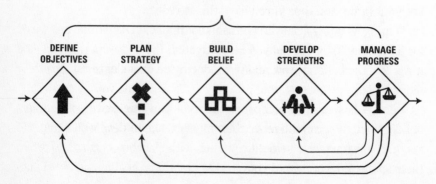

| DEFINE OBJECTIVES | PLAN STRATEGY | BUILD BELIEF | DEVELOP STRENGTHS | MANAGE PROGRESS |

Analyze almost any goal you've ever set and reached, and you'll discover that you either consciously or unconsciously followed these steps.

In this system, I've brought all the elements of goal achievement together. All you have to do is add sufficient desire and action to make it work for you. Though at first you may not understand the power of this system, follow it faithfully over a period of time and you'll be astounded at the results.

Taking Action

In order to get into action, you'll need a pad of paper and a pen or pencil. Read the following questions and write responses to the ones that are most meaningful to you. Skip over the rest.

I suggest that you make quick decisions as you answer the important questions. You can change any of your responses tomorrow. So don't put a lot of pressure on yourself to have the right answer.

1. How much would you like to weigh?
2. What specific sales skills would you like to develop?
3. What specific habit would you like to develop?
4. What specific habit would you like to break?
5. What personality trait would you like to develop?
6. What kind of home would you like to own?
7. What improvement would you like to make in your present home?
8. What would you like to do on your next vacation?
9. How would you like to communicate with family members?
10. How would you like to communicate with coworkers?
11. What new office would you like to enjoy?
12. What new position would you like to attain?
13. What new honor would you like to receive?
14. What specific person would you like to have as a closer friend?
15. What improvement in your physical condition would you like to make?
16. What professional or occupational skills would you like to strengthen?
17. What artistic or creative talent would you like to develop?
18. What kind of person would you like to marry?
19. What new hobby would you like to begin?

20. What new activity would you like to begin?
21. What one thing could you do to add more enjoyment to your life?
22. What one goal could you reach that would solve a specific problem you now have?
23. What one goal could you reach that would lessen tension or stress in your life?
24. What one activity could you do that would relieve pressure or worry?
25. What study habits would you like to acquire?
26. What grade-point average would you like to earn?
27. What additional education would you like to have?
28. What physical activity would you like to start?
29. How much money would you like to save each pay period?
30. What specific financial habit would you like to develop?
31. What debts would you like to pay off?
32. How much money would you like to have each month when you retire?
33. How much money would you like to leave your family in case of an unexpected death?
34. What charitable contributions would you like to make?
35. How much merchandise, goods, or services would you like to sell? Each month, quarter, year?
36. What specific client relationships would you like to strengthen?
37. What would you like to do for your place of worship?
38. What would you like to do for your community?
39. What civic interest or public service would you like to be involved in?
40. How would you like others to describe you?
41. What image would you like to communicate to others?
42. What specific actions can you take to build up your family members?
43. What family activities can you start doing?
44. What common interests can you plan to involve yourself with other family members?
45. What spiritual goals would you like to reach?
46. What spiritual qualities would you like to develop?
47. What other things would you like to have happen to you in the next year?

Now that you've written answers to the ones that are meaningful to you, here's what I want you to do.

STEP 1. Please review your written responses to the questions. Reflect on your answers. Mark the six most important ones by looking over all your responses and selecting the one *most* important goal, the *next* most important goal, and so on.

STEP 2. When you've selected the six most important goals, look at each one and write down a time limit or date by which you want to achieve the goal. Give yourself plenty of time. Nothing happens overnight—although many of your goals will come into reality before you expect them to. But for now, be realistic about your target dates.

STEP 3. When you've written target dates beside each of your goals, turn them into definite statements like this:
   "By (date), I'll (verb) (goal)."
   Let me give you some examples.

   "By May 15, I'll weigh 180 pounds."

   "By July 31, I'll average sales of $200,000 per month."

   "Beginning January 1, I'll save 10 percent of my income each
      month."

   "By September 15, I'll close the XYZ account."

Writing your goals this way puts them in the form of active self-suggestions.

STEP 4. When you have all six goals written as statements, get six index cards. On each card write a goal statement on one side. You might even write them in exciting colors—maybe each in a different one. After writing them on the cards, put a rubber band around them. You're going to carry the cards with you and read them each day.

YOUR DESIRED END RESULTS A goal is a statement of your desired end result, or what you want to happen at different intervals in your future.

When I've asked people about their goals, I get less than specific responses, such as "My goal is to lose some weight!" or "My goal is to sell more!" Or, "My goal is to make more money" or "My goal is to get a larger home!" or "My goal is to take more time with my family."

Responses like these have a common problem—they aren't specific. They contain words like *more, better, good, some,* and *larger,* which keep your statements from being goal-specific. So please watch out for these and other words that do the same. In the goal-setting seminars that I conduct, I start participants off by having them write this statement down: "A goal is a statement of the desired end result!"

Planning Strategy

The second step of our Goal Achievement System is planning strategy. Sometimes this can be done carefully in advance; other times we have to spend time discovering it.

There are basically two kinds of goals.

1. The strategy or steps of achievement are known and have to be taken.
2. The strategy or steps are unknown and have to be discovered.

For some goals, such as building a home, it's pretty simple to plan your strategy. You hire a builder or an architect to design a plan and then you execute it. Other goals, such as getting a better job or developing spiritual values, make planning a strategy more difficult because you're often not sure what exactly you'll have to do to reach them.

There are other factors that influence your goal-planning strategy. An important one: planning is a left-brain, logical exercise that requires some concrete organizational ability, but generating the power to reach goals is usually a right-brain, creative activity—dreaming, believing, and visualizing goal attainment. Often these dimensions don't exist equally in the same person.

In my experience, people who get emotionally charged about new goals often have problems making clear plans. Many are so action-oriented that they go off in all directions. I've also observed that few people will actually sit down and initiate a goal strategy. Another interesting trait I've witnessed is that those left-brain, detail-minded people who do plot out elaborate goal plans often enjoy *designing* the plan more than *working it out.* Paralysis by analysis.

STRATEGY QUESTIONS TO ASK Here are four simple questions that will help you get your planning job done:

1. What's my target date to reach this goal?
2. How can I break my goal down into subgoals or incremental steps?
3. What different activity levels will it take to reach this sales goal?
4. What activities can I perform today?

Answering these questions will get you a long way down the road in goal planning. They address both the long and short term and bring the reality of goal achievement into the present.

Break down your goals into subgoals or incremental steps. Your goal may be to sell a specific amount each month, or to retire, or to have a specific net worth. Or it may be to sell larger accounts or to lose twenty-five pounds. All of these goals can be broken down into incremental steps. Then as each step is realized, you move toward your larger goals.

PROGRAM YOUR "I AM" TO REVEAL YOUR PLAN TO YOUR "I THINK" There are some goals for which you can't plan, because they result from a creative idea. You must have "lightbulb" experiences for these goals to be achieved. In other words, your "I Think" is working in harmony with your "I Am." Your unconscious Creative Mechanism combines with your experience, knowledge, and inner beliefs and—zap—you wake up in the middle of the night and the way to reach your goal flashes into your mind. Maybe you're jogging, or in traffic, and your mind is on something totally unrelated to your goals. Suddenly the answer appears.

This answer, or creative idea, didn't pop into your consciousness because you laid out logical plans. It did so because a powerful Goal-Seeking Mechanism inside your "I Am" was also working on the goal. This process gives birth to hunches, flashes of insight, and creative discoveries.

One evening in 1980 I was having dinner with W. Clement Stone in his Chicago home. He talked a great deal about his work with Napoleon Hill, author of the classic work *Think and Grow Rich.* It seemed that the book had been finished with only a working title. The publisher called Hill and told him that they were going to press the next morning and that if he didn't have a title, the publisher would name it.

"What will you name it?" he asked.

The publisher responded, *"Use Your Noodle to Get the Boodle!"*

"You can't be serious," Hill frantically shot back.

"Well, that's what it'll be tomorrow unless you come up with a better one."

Hill was panic-stricken at this awful title.

Before going to sleep he thought hard about a new title. He thought how bad *Use Your Noodle to Get the Boodle* was. His stress level was high.

Early the next morning, he awoke with the clear thought, *Think and Grow Rich,* and the rest is history. The book touched millions of lives, and over sixty years later it's still selling. It's interesting how the answers often pop into our minds at the minute we must have them.

Building Belief in Your Goals

This step is the critical one for goal achievement to take place. How do we go about building belief that we can actually reach our goals? How can we expand our belief boundaries to accommodate our new goals?

There are basically four ways to do this:

1. Self-Suggestion
2. Visualization
3. Graphic representation
4. Environmental influences

SELF-SUGGESTION Self-suggestions are positive statements we repeatedly make to ourselves. We do it with emotion and repetition, then eventually reprogram our unconscious beliefs in our "I Am" dimension. We develop a new way of thinking.

Several years ago I admitted that I needed to lose some weight. *Okay, I said to myself, but that isn't very specific. How much would I like to weigh?* I thought about it and set a goal of 190. At the time I weighed almost 220.

So I began saying the affirmation, "I weigh 190 pounds and eat accordingly!" I repeated it over and over. Nothing happened the first two or three weeks, but after that things quickly started changing. My appetite decreased. I didn't want sweets anymore. I focused on what I wanted to end up weighing rather than dwelling on the deprivation that I'd surely have to undergo. And in 120 days or so, I weighed 190 pounds.

It was all a matter of painting a new picture in my "I Am." Repeated verbal commands, propelled by strong desire or emotion, will program new beliefs in your "I Am." These then trigger specific actions to carry out these new mental images.

VISUALIZATION Visualization is another method of reaching and then planting new pictures in your "I Am."

We're constantly projecting pictures on the screens of our minds. The trick is to consciously choose healthy, wholesome images on which to center your thoughts. But what do many people do when they set goals? Often they center their thoughts on what could go *wrong* rather than on what could go *right,* on what they don't want to happen rather than what they do want to occur.

The pictures you choose, either voluntarily or involuntarily, become targets for your Goal-Seeking Mechanism to carry out for you. Remember, this powerful Creative Mechanism is impartial—it simply carries out the programming you give it with your thoughts. It makes no judgments as to what should or should not happen in your life. This is for your values either to allow or override.

If your thoughts are focused on fear or anxiety or what could go wrong in the pursuit of your goals, these thoughts will become the targets of your inner Goal-Seeking Mechanism, which will steer you to them and help them become realities. This will happen to the extent of the intensity of your mental pictures. Knowing this, you should carefully choose the pictures you hold in your mind.

It's also important to know that the unconscious "I Am" is more open to programming in a relaxed state than a wide-awake one: moments before you go to sleep; the half-awake time before you arise in the mornings; times of reverie when you're relaxing in the sun or in your most comfortable chair; times when your active, conscious "I Think" isn't whirling, churning, turning, or burning.

One of my mentors, W. Clement Stone, had the habit of taking a slow, relaxing bath early in the morning. Isolated from any interruptions, he would allow the hot water to speed him into a stressless state where he would review his goals and plans for the upcoming day. He carried out this ritual for many years, having trained his mind to respond and focus on his plans for the day and the rewards he would enjoy when certain goals were reached. It was often in this process that the plan, or the means whereby he could reach his goals, was sent to his conscious mind.

In his classic *Psycho-Cybernetics,* Maxwell Maltz pointed this out: "Physical relaxation, when practiced daily, brings about an accompanying mental relaxation and a relaxed attitude then enables us to consciously control our automatic mechanism. Physical relaxation has a powerful influence, dehypnotizing us from negative attitudes and reaction patterns."

Your goals will see the reality faster as you learn to spend time each day relaxing and visualizing their attainment as well as the rewards you'll enjoy at that point.

GRAPHIC EXPOSURE Another method of building belief that your goals can become realities is graphic exposure: keeping pictures, words, slogans, or symbols that remind you of your goals.

Many people in my courses have told me of cutting out pictures of a new automobile, house, boat, or other tangible item that they wanted to get. They'd look at it several times each day, visualizing themselves already having it and enjoying it. And in what appeared to be no time at all, they found a way to get it.

ENVIRONMENTAL INFLUENCES The fourth way to build belief in your goals is to structure supportive environmental influences. These are the people, places, or things that influence our success. We usually conform to our environment, because it has a powerful influence on us.

Here are some suggestions that will help you structure supportive environmental influences:

1. Carefully choose the people with whom you associate. Choose people who are performing or living on the level at which you'd like to perform or live.

2. Choose an environment where you can grow and have unlimited opportunities to learn.

3. Expose yourself to other people's prosperity by driving through wealthy neighborhoods. Visit stores, art galleries, or study good architecture.

4. Spend time with wise, discerning people. Read good literature. Read biographies of wise, successful people. Study the words of wisdom in the Bible.

Prosperity is first a state of mind; it then translates itself into reality. These environmental influences can help develop greater prosperity consciousness.

I love to drive through upscale neighborhoods and look at the homes. When I first began to do this years ago, actually living in one was totally outside my own belief system. As I'd drive by these homes and go into upscale shops it reminded me that a lot of people had mentally accepted that high level of prosperity. I told myself that this means it's possible. And if it's possible for them, it's possible for me, too. This experience always has a very positive influence on my own belief system.

Spending time with wise, spiritually discerning people also has a very positive influence on our prosperity thinking. It helps us broaden our thinking and sort out our own views.

How can you stretch your thinking and understanding?

Developing Strengths to Reach Your Goals

Often, before a goal can be reached, we must develop some personal strengths. The same is true in pursuing corporate or organizational goals. Developing strengths is simply part of the price.

During goal-achievement seminars and courses over the years, I've asked participants to assess the following strengths:

1. Attitudes
2. Habits
3. Skills
4. Specialized knowledge

ATTITUDES Our attitudes are how we think—about ourselves, about others, about situations and circumstances. It's a mind-set, a belief system, and a viewpoint. We commonly define attitudes as positive or negative, but they're much more complex than that. They are the product of our education, experiences, culture, and heritage, as well as the training, mentoring, and modeling we receive from others.

HABITS A habit is an automatic response, done unconsciously, instinctively, without thinking. We're all creatures of habit, from the way we brush our teeth, comb our hair, and put on our shoes in the morning, to the way we do our jobs. Good habits cause good results; bad ones cause bad results.

Success is usually the result of certain habits. Once a habit is formed, our automatic mechanism takes over and unconsciously causes us to perform in a habitual way in different situations. Most successful people have developed good time-management habits. Procrastination, indecisiveness, and inaction are weak habits that can be changed.

It usually takes a minimum of twenty-one days of practicing an action before a habit emerges. It's with your "I Think" that you practice the actions; then, with repetition and time lapse, your "I Am" is programmed! Habits are broken the same way.

What habits will it take to reach your goals? What habits will you have to break? With what will you replace them? As you review your goals, ask yourself these questions and record your responses. This process can open the doors to your new goals.

SKILLS Skills are developed abilities, such as reading, writing, and arithmetic. Playing golf, painting a picture, sewing a button on a shirt, performing a root canal, doing laser surgery to remove a cataract, and riding a bicycle are all skills.

In order to reach your goals, you'll have to develop skills, regardless of whether your goal is to be a legal secretary, accountant, computer programmer, or auto technician.

A good question, then, is, What skills must I develop in order to reach my goals? The skills you define will then become subgoals.

SPECIALIZED KNOWLEDGE The fourth strength you'll have to develop in order to reach your goals is specialized knowledge.

As our society becomes more technologically complex, specialized knowledge becomes more important. Today, for instance, you'll probably have to have much more specialized knowledge than you did ten years ago. You must know more about your clients' businesses in order to effectively compete in your marketplace. You must know much more about technology to perform your job well.

Many goals demand specialized knowledge. How about yours? What specialized knowledge will reaching your sales goals demand? Again, it will be helpful for you to write them down. Then, if you're serious about reaching your goals, you'll find a way to gain the specialized knowledge you'll need.

Managing Your Goal Progress

In order to evaluate and manage your progress, here are four Action Guides:

1. Review goals
2. Proceed
3. Revise
4. Recycle

Let's consider each step. You'll see how easy they are and how they fit into our system.

REVIEW GOALS Review your goals by asking yourself some questions:

1. Where am I with this goal—what is my progress?
2. Are all my goals still important to me?
3. How can I best use my time?
4. What subgoals should I have already reached to take me to my main goals?

As you review your goals, you'll discover only three appropriate responses: proceed, revise, or recycle.

PROCEED You'll *proceed* with your goal if you still want to achieve it, believe that it's possible, and are willing to keep developing the strengths to reach it—in other words, your goal is still important to you. Maybe you haven't had enough time. So you keep building belief and developing the strengths you need.

REVISE Another appropriate response after you review your goals is to *revise* them. I'm always amazed at how fast some goals become realized. I often look back at the booklets in which I've written down goals. Most of them have happened—and often sooner than I expected.

I also discover that many of my goals had to be revised. They had to be revised either up or down. Often I find that after setting and working on goals for a while, that they aren't consistent with my values, my priorities, or some of my other goals. For these reasons, I need to revise them. I rewrite them and keep working on the system—planning strategy, building belief, developing strengths, and managing progress.

RECYCLE Often when you review your goals you discover that you need to *recycle*. This involves redefining your goals and going back through your Goal Achievement System. Do the following:

1. Begin with new goals
2. Plan strategy
3. Build belief
4. Develop strengths
5. Manage progress

You may also recycle when you've had a lapse of interest or have once set a goal and later stalled out. It's common to set a goal, be serious about it for a while, and then lose interest. Perhaps new events cause it to slip from your priorities, then later you get excited about it again.

Look at It as a System

The Goal Achievement System I've presented is powerful and workable. When you follow the system and manage your progress, you'll be amazed at how quickly some of your goals materialize. It has built-in checks, balances, and policing agents. It has its own internal guidance systems. It's fully functioning; all you have to do is punch the start-up button, activate, maintain the system, and it'll work for you.

I've conducted enough courses and seminars in goal setting to know about getting people to follow this system. One common response is, *Yeah, well, this may all be true, but there's more to life than just reaching material goals!* I agree; there's more to life than cars, houses, clothes, and money. I'll be the first to admit it. Spiritual dimensions and family and personal relationships are infinitely more important. But these inner qualities are also goals, and you can use this system to attain them.

Practice Until the Steps Are Automatic

I'll admit this five-step system looks mechanical, with many rules and guidelines, but I've designed it that way for a purpose. The reason is so nothing is left to chance, that we cover all of the bases.

I know from experience that if you follow this system to the letter you'll experience success. When you do, you'll emotionally believe in the process. Then, with time and experience, the whole Goal Achievement System will become automatic. You'll perform many of the steps unconsciously.

With repetition you'll instinctively begin to think and act in a goal-focused way.

HOW TO GAIN THE MOST FROM THIS CHAPTER

Abundance begins as a state of mind that can be developed over time, by doing a few simple actions.

Your Goal-Seeking Mechanism is your onboard computer that unconsciously steers you to the goals or targets you set for it. Understand the power and function of this mechanism and you'll see how the Goal Achievement System is the blueprint. The system gives you a process on which to focus your powerful Goal-Seeking Mechanism.

In order to benefit from the power of this chapter, here are some action steps to follow:

1. Read and digest the chapter, and focus on the content for a week.
2. Follow the instructions, set some specific goals, and go through the Goal Achievement System.
3. Particularly follow my suggestions for building belief in your goals. Write affirmations on cards and place them where they'll serve as daily reminders. Build your own goal poster and look at it often.

The Goal Achievement System, when faithfully practiced, can gradually lift you from where you are and take you to where you want to go. It can be a way of life for you—working deeper and more smoothly as you get more and more proficient at doing it.

Repeat this self-suggestion to yourself over and over this week: "Abundance is all around me—just waiting to enter my life when I give sufficient value to others."

5 SETTING GOALS FOR THE FUTURE YOU

Assessment

Please take a few moments and check off the number that best describes your present beliefs, boundaries, or behaviors. Use these descriptors as guidelines.

5–Always true, without exception
4–Mostly true
3–True more often than not
2–True only part of the time
1–True only occasionally

1. I rarely set sales goals.	5 4 3 2 1	1 2 3 4 5	1. I continually set goals for higher sales.
2. I'm mostly concerned with not failing.	5 4 3 2 1	1 2 3 4 5	2. I have an abundance mentality.
3. I don't allow myself to think of goals that I might not reach.	5 4 3 2 1	1 2 3 4 5	3. I think in terms of higher success possibilities.

4. My goal strategies often contain words like *good, some, better, increased, more,* etc.	5 4 3 2 1	1 2 3 4 5	4. My goals are specifically stated in terms of end results.
5. If I don't see a clear path to a goal, I don't continue to work on it.	5 4 3 2 1	1 2 3 4 5	5. I keep focused on a goal even though I'm not sure how to reach it.
6. I only associate with people who are reaching my level of goals, or lower.	5 4 3 2 1	1 2 3 4 5	6. I carefully associate with people who are reaching goals I'd like to be reaching.
7. I don't seem to have the ability to do goal planning.	5 4 3 2 1	1 2 3 4 5	7. I carefully plan for how to reach my goals, then adjust and revise as needed.
8. I tend to give up on a goal when problems or uncertainties arise.	5 4 3 2 1	1 2 3 4 5	8. I persist in my pursuit of goals despite any roadblocks or temporary defeats.
9. I've failed at reaching goals in the past, and just don't want to suffer any disappointment again.	5 4 3 2 1	1 2 3 4 5	9. I'm constantly visualizing the rewards I'll give myself when I reach my goals.

- Add up the numbers in the right-hand column. _____
- Add up the numbers in the left-hand column. _____
- Subtract the left-hand column total from the right-hand column total and score yourself. _____

Assessments scoring guide is on page 35.

Keeping Score—Chapter 5

Behavior that gets evaluated, gets improved.

On a scale of 1–10, please evaluate how well you practiced the following behaviors this week.

	S	M	T	W	T	F	S
1. I set and/or reviewed my goals today.							
2. I planned and/or reviewed my strategy today.							
3. I built belief today by: self-suggestions, visualizations, graphic exposure, or environmental influences.							
4. I developed a strength today: attitudes, habits, skills, or specialized knowledge.							
5. I managed my goal process today: review goals, proceed, revise, or recycle.							
6. I did one activity today that focused my mind on abundance.							
Total Each Day							

6 Creativity

Discovering Your Creative Goal-Seeking Mechanism

PAUL RIVIERE, OF NASHVILLE, TENNESSEE, WAS ALREADY a very high-producing, $10 million real estate agent before he caught fire.

After he enrolled in our Integrity Selling course and implemented its processes, his sales immediately jumped 25 percent. And as is the case for all high achievers, the more successful he became, the more room for increased success he discovered.

Then, he did a most creative thing. He began inviting all the people who purchased homes from him each month to come to his home for an elegant dinner prepared by his wife, Carolyn. He asked each one to bring something that they'd read or experienced and share it with the group after dinner.

When I interviewed one of his monthly guests, she couldn't quit talking about how nice and unexpected it was. She praised the sincerity and hospitality of Paul and Carolyn with words like, "a heart for people," "high values," and "highly professional."

"Paul and Carolyn's home radiates love, stability, and respectability. Paul takes his business way past business," his guest remarked. "He doesn't see it as a job; he sees it as a ministry. He has a clear purpose—to give the most value to his clients."

Is it any wonder why Paul enjoys such a huge business? What clients wouldn't want their friends and family to choose him to buy or sell their home?

Creativity, not following the normal way real estate salespeople attempt to sell homes: Paul sells by not trying to sell, but by serving people.

Everyone is endowed with the gift of creativity—a powerful Creative Mechanism was installed in each of us before birth. Some of us focus this powerful mechanism on basic survival, while others discover it and allow it to lead them into all kinds of higher achievement—intellectual, artistic, material, emotional, spiritual, and social.

Many people go through life never knowing they have a highly efficient Creative Mechanism within them. Others may get an occasional glimpse of it but get trapped into using it to reach only survival goals. Great people— artists, musicians, writers, problem solvers, talented people of all callings—have consciously or unconsciously discovered this mechanism and then chosen to develop, polish, and actualize it. Because of this we have beautiful symphonies, art, architecture, medical cures, and a host of other discoveries that advance our society and elevate the human condition.

Great salespeople do the same thing. They seek ways to sell and serve their customers on higher than average levels. Since this mechanism is a dimension of divinity within us, it has no limits, except those we place on ourselves through our own self-imposed belief boundaries. Accept this fact, and it'll keep you scratching your head and wondering about your limits.

The practical circumstances of your life can easily keep you blinded from your actual potential, unless, of course, you come to grips with the truth about yourself.

The Truth About You

The truth about you is that you have the inner creative ability to reach any goal that:

1. You can imagine
2. You internally view as being possible
3. You feel worthy of receiving
4. Doesn't conflict with your values
5. You're willing to make a commitment to work on and see through to fulfillment.

Remember, Thomas Edison was kicked out of school after a short time in the first grade. Not much formal education for one of the greatest contributors to the 19th and 20th century, was it? His teachers told his parents that he was "addled" and incapable of learning and that any formal education would be wasted on him.

Let's hear it for "addled"!

I'm always amazed at what happens to people in our courses when we help them discover and access their creative powers. We have people achieve such goals as getting new clients, losing weight, getting new homes, and discovering talents that have previously lain dormant within them.

I recently attended the graduation of one of our Managing Goal Achievement® courses in a YWCA for abused women. Each of the participants had chosen to leave their abuser and enter a special program. In one of the early sessions, one person noticed another doodling on a piece of paper and complimented her on her artistic abilities, which because of her low self-esteem, she denied having.

Another person in the class was a Realtor and introduced her to a builder who needed house renderings done. By the end of the course, this person was earning money with her renderings. She discovered a highly developed artistic talent that had been previously locked up.

I speak from experience when I say that you have the inner creative ability to achieve any goal you deeply desire, view possible, feel you deserve to enjoy, and are willing to work and see through. This is the truth about you.

To guard this truth from yourself, you must pull up the drawbridge of your mind, keeping out destructive forces that might invade your dreams and goals. You must protect and nurture your incredibly valuable beliefs about your success possibilities.

Building Your Own Belief in the Size Goals You Can Reach

I've noted this earlier, but perhaps the most profound thing I've learned about people in all my years of human development is that the goals we reach are always consistent with our inner beliefs about who we are, what's possible for us to achieve, and what we deserve to have. Every time I think or say this I take it to a deeper level of understanding.

Until these deep-rooted internal pictures change, our achievements will pretty much stay the same. But expand these beliefs on the inside and higher success happens quickly on the outside. Albert Einstein once remarked, "The level of thinking that got you to the present will not take you into the future."

Higher achievement demands growth and change!

A Sense of Worthiness

Most important, higher achievement involves developing a sense of worthiness. We most internally feel that we deserve higher and broader success.

As I've listened to tens of thousands of people in my development courses, I've become completely convinced that our greatest success barrier is undervaluing our real selves. Rather than feelings of arrogance, egotism, or over-confidence, we need a total understanding of our actual capacities for higher success and creative expression, which leads to humility and self-respect.

For seven years before his death, I worked with Maxwell Maltz, author of *Psycho-Cybernetics*. He wrote the following in this masterpiece as a conclusion to his whole message:

> Finally, let us not limit our acceptance of life by our own feelings of unworthiness. God has offered us forgiveness and the peace of mind and happiness that comes from self-acceptance. It is an insult to our Creator to turn our back upon these gifts or to say that His creation—man—is so unclean that he is not worthy, or important, or capable.

Most religions teach that "the laborer is worthy of his hire." "When we sow plenty, we should reap plenty."

To expect to give much, and not receive a reciprocal amount, is wrong. This limited thinking blocks our creative channels, and clogs our passages to the success we deserve when we have freely given of ourselves.

But just knowing how isn't enough. It takes more. It takes action. This is why I have included numerous Action Guides in each chapter.

Stripping Away External Negative and Limiting Influences

The third strategy that must be taken in order to grow and enjoy higher goals is to strip away external negative influences that tend to stall you and keep you exactly where you are now.

Do you have people in your life who seem to think that their sole purpose is to rein you in and keep your life from getting out of hand? People who continually remind you of your past failures or defeats? Who pass judgment on your actions, choices, and decisions? Who love to tell you why things won't work or can't be done?

Are you working around negative people who sap your creative energies? Whose success seems to be measured by your failures? Is your present environment—where you live, where you work, what you do with your time—limiting your ability to expand your life?

Most of us do have people, places, or things in our lives that make it difficult to move into expanded levels of achievement. If you have these, it's important to change them, block them out, or remove yourself from them. At least develop support systems that help neutralize their negative influences.

But let's face it: making such decisions can be very difficult or even painful. When you do, though, you can often free yourself of clutter and damaging effects.

A Poverty Consciousness

Many people don't think in terms of abundance but of scarcity and limitations, and therefore they have a *poverty consciousness*. They unconsciously focus on why they can't achieve goals, rather than why they can. They've been conditioned to watch out for the potholes of life, rather than to enjoy the unfolding beautiful scenery. While we can't escape our past conditioning, we can escape the entanglements of it.

Escape begins with an understanding that prosperity is a birthright we have; we then set out to claim it.

It seems to me that if I use my unique God-given talents to the extent that I'm capable, then in this process I'll create a lot of value for a lot of people. Under the Law of Reciprocity, that we always get back what we give in multiplied measures, this strategy guarantees I'll enjoy abundance—as a consequence of the abundance I help create for others. To me this is entirely consistent with God's laws of sowing and reaping.

Let me say again that when I speak of abundance, I know it can take many forms—money, self-esteem, relationships, respect, recognition, appreciation, love, joy, peace. There are many forms of payment for creating high value, and all of us want different forms of compensation.

Nature's law is that seeds reproduce after their kind, and we always receive back in increased amounts the good seeds we sow—especially when we give for the simple joy of giving. Another paradox is that we enjoy all this in increased measures when we focus on sowing the right seeds rather than just focusing only on the harvest.

Admittedly, this thinking flies into the face of many people's and organizations' self-focused natures. Too often we focus only on profit or income goals, rather than the service we can give or the value we can create that would then yield the profit. Profits are the natural result of creating value for people and managing our resources well. So profit goals are only reached by achieving other productivity goals.

This book is written not just to share sales skills with you, but to help you develop an ever-increasing prosperity consciousness so you can unconsciously focus on the abundance that's available to you. Once your "I Am" accepts the picture of expanded prosperity, your sales will quickly go up to fill this new picture.

To understand how you can do this, let me introduce you to one of your inner miracles.

The Miracle of Your Creative Mechanism

You are a bundle of several miracles that are housed in your "I Am."

Inside your "I Am" resides a host of Miracle Mechanisms. They regulate your heartbeat, your body temperature, your lymphatic flow, your weight, and your emotional and physical controls.

One of these miracles is your inner Creative Mechanism. This sends your conscious mind hunches, insights, and answers. It allows you to come up with new solutions to problems and to put new combinations of existing materials together and form something new.

This Creative Mechanism also becomes a Goal-Seeking Mechanism that can silently steer you to whatever goals you select.

A Goal-Seeking Mechanism

When you have clear goals or targets you think are possible for you to achieve and you feel worthy of having, this Goal-Seeking Mechanism silently and unconsciously steers you toward them. It works in the most common, everyday functions like putting on your shoes, brushing your teeth, or driving to work. You have a goal—to get to work or get dressed—and your unconscious mechanism takes over and directs the necessary physical and mental functions in order to help you reach your goal.

I'm always amazed at the mysterious ways that goals become realities for our course members. I've heard story after story of how people got new homes in neighborhoods that they could have only imagined. I'll never forget doing a seminar in Detroit, Michigan, some time back. A man who had been in a course of mine in Texas a few years earlier came to tell me his story. He explained that in the course he had set a goal to get a house that was significantly beyond his financial means. He even cut out a picture of his dream house—an English Tudor style. He showed us the picture he had taped on his pocket goal planner.

With a sparkle in his eyes, he asked me, "May I buy you dinner tonight—I want to show you my new home."

After the session, he drove me to his new home, stopping first in front of it, and again showed me the picture that he had cut out of a magazine long before he found the home. The similarity was incredible.

He then explained to me how he found it and how he was able to afford it.

He first saw the home after moving to Detroit. He drove by to look at it time after time, and knocked on the door once to ask if it was for sale. He found out that it wasn't, but got acquainted with the elderly couple who owned it and kept going by to visit with them. Months later, the wife in the house passed away and the husband wanted to move to live with a daughter. He wanted my friend's family to have the house, so he reduced the price and made financial arrangements so they could afford it.

I've heard many, many similar stories of how, when a goal is set, mysterious events happen to make the goal a reality.

We see this same magnetic power in sports.

At the crack of a bat, the center fielder runs to a point where the ball will fall. With only a fraction of a second to reach it, how did he know where it would go? A quarterback drops back three steps, plants his foot, looks, and throws the football at a point where a receiver will be in two or three seconds. How did he know just where to place the ball? In three seconds how could he have gone through the necessary mathematical calculations? How could he have factored in the speed of the receiver, the speed of the ball, the wind or barometric pressure? He couldn't have. He didn't have time to do all this. Or could he?

A better way to say it is that these players couldn't have gone through the conscious mental calculations in their "I Think." They did, though, go through the mental calculations unconsciously in their "I Am" dimensions. Something within them knew exactly when and how to judge or throw the ball. They were able to do these complex, unconscious calculations after programming their "I Am" dimension through mental rehearsal, practice, repetition, feedback, and coaching.

Once a clear picture or pattern of the desired level of performance is clear in a player's "I Am," then he or she, without consciously thinking through it, simply executes. Something within them takes over and marvelously guides their muscles and reflexes so that the right result takes place.

Hunches, Intuition, Ideas Sent to Your "I Think"

Your Goal-Seeking Mechanism also works teleologically. It works unconsciously to seek out specific targets. When you have goal clarity, or have defined specific, measurable targets, this mechanism acts as a guidance system to steer you to them.

Often when you set a sales goal, the target is known but the strategy to get there isn't. So you begin a series of actions. Some advance you toward your goal, others get you nowhere. You usually have to take corrective measures as you're moving toward your target or goal. You gradually find out what will work and what won't. Almost all goals require feedback and corrective actions in order to reach them.

Your corrections only become clear and manageable when you have a goal or target on which to direct your efforts. Focusing on the goal helps you monitor your progress and make needed changes, or corrections, that are necessary to reach it.

In all goal achievement, we must keep asking, "What is my goal and what must I do to reach it?" Your inner guidance system will then reveal the needed correction of your course.

Let's look at the model below to get a clear picture of what I'm saying.

Your "I Think" selects a goal, and the resources in your "I Am" go to work to steer you to it, when your "I Am" believes it to be possible. If your "I Am" believes that it is, it also triggers emotions of confidence, enthusiasm, energy, hope, worthiness, and achievement drive. If you don't internally believe the goal is possible, or if it's inconsistent with your values or feelings of worthiness, then feelings of disbelief, frustration, and inadequacy are triggered in your "I Feel."

In other words, success demands the integration of your "I Think" and your "I Am" for your "I Feel" to be positive.

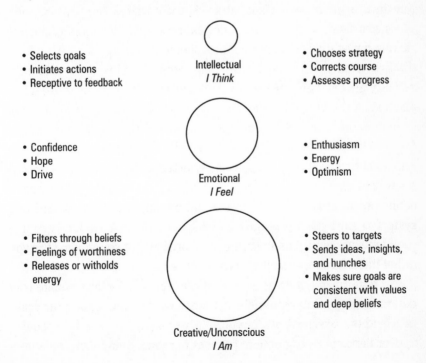

• Selects goals   Intellectual   • Chooses strategy
• Initiates actions   *I Think*   • Corrects course
• Receptive to feedback   • Assesses progress

• Confidence   • Enthusiasm
• Hope   • Energy
• Drive   Emotional   • Optimism
                 I Feel

• Filters through beliefs   • Steers to targets
• Feelings of worthiness   • Sends ideas, insights,
• Releases or witholds   and hunches
  energy   • Makes sure goals are
                               consistent with values
                               and deep beliefs

Creative/Unconscious
I Am

Remember, your "I Think" is constantly interacting with your "I Am," and how they connect or disconnect then triggers emotions in your "I Feel."

As you continue to study this concept you'll take it to increasingly deeper levels of understanding.

Your "I Think" Selects Goals

It's with your conscious mind that you decide on certain goals, or, by default, you choose not to have any. You exercise conscious willpower to get you started and initiate the necessary actions to carry out your goal strategy.

When you set goals, and to the degree that you're seriously committed to their attainment, you automatically trigger certain emotions.

Have you ever set a goal that you internally knew you wouldn't reach? Most of us have done this from time to time. New Year's resolutions are one example. They often last about as long as the bubbles in the champagne do.

I've seen many salespeople set goals that pleased their managers and got them momentary applause from their associates, but because their goals were beyond their beliefs, they didn't achieve them. Lots of people do this, and it's devastating to their self-confidence.

How Your "I Feel" Reacts to the Goals You Set

Let's keep thinking that whenever your "I Think" sets a goal, the programming in your "I Am" unconsciously evaluates its possibilities and triggers emotions in your "I Feel." Then whatever positive or negative emotions that are triggered powerfully influence your attainment of the goals you set.

Before I explain more about this, let me emphasize that your inner beliefs become the filters through which your goals flow. It's here that they either pass through with approval or they get shot down. They're either unconsciously accepted as possible or rejected.

No goal, in and of itself, is impossible. What becomes possible isn't determined by what's possible for other people, but what your inner beliefs think to be possible for you.

Our lifetime of programming causes our inner self-beliefs and views of our possibilities to be formed. And just as it took time for them to be formed, so it takes time to change them. So don't get too impatient as you work on changing some of the not-so-true beliefs that have been limiting you. Make discovering the truth about yourself—that you are capable of achieving any goal that you believe to be possible—a lifelong development process.

Keep reminding yourself of this truth.

Your Goal-Seeking Mechanism Helps

Your inner mechanism will help you reach whatever goals you feed it— whether they're negative or positive, healthy or unhealthy, good or bad.

The objects of your innermost desires, or fears, become the real focus of your Goal-Seeking Mechanism. Strong thoughts or fears on which you choose to focus your mental energy become targets for your inner mechanism to help you reach.

The prophet Job lamented, "The thing I feared has come upon me." This is good psychology. The thing you fear becomes a goal for your Goal-Seeking Mechanism to bring into existence. Whatever mental or emotional pictures we hold in our minds, our powerful mechanism steers us to them.

Here are some common fear-goals that salespeople inadvertently set.

- "I can't sell on that high level."
- "I'm afraid I can't make this quota."
- "I probably can't get an appointment with the decision makers."
- "The economy is bad."
- "Decision makers don't want to see me on Mondays or Fridays."

You can probably pick out more limiting thoughts that salespeople have.

There's a big problem here. What you feed your mind, you become. Whether you unconsciously focus on positive, constructive goals, or negative, destructive ones, your mechanism will serve you efficiently by silently steering you to them. It operates impersonally, and without evaluating the rightness or wrongness of your goals. In many cases your deepest desires drive this inner mechanism; at other times your values do. Your choices determine the dominant driver. You can exercise discipline and select productive, healthy goals, or you can allow your fears, limiting beliefs, or unhealthy desires to rule.

Knowing this about the mind should give us great cause for alarm about the real thoughts we have and our desires of the heart. But it can also free us and catapult us to higher, more productive goals—when we choose to take charge of our lives.

We have choices each moment.

The Power of Inner Beliefs About Yourself

Your deep feelings of worthiness or unworthiness, possibilities or impossibilities, will either help you carry out the goals you constantly set, or else sabotage them in the most subtle and creative ways. The results will be consistent with your inner beliefs.

I see people who grew up with healthy nurturing from their parents. They enjoyed much positive reinforcement, love, and encouragement, and they reached high goals. Analyze them and you'll find they just naturally expect to win. They were conditioned by their early nurturing to feel adequate and valuable. They had healthy views of themselves and what they were worthy of enjoying. Reaching high goals is just a logical manifestation of their inner beliefs and feelings of value.

I see other people for whom the opposite happens. Their low self-opinions seem to block sustained success, regardless of how hard they try.

This reminds me of a person who was a very good friend of mine. He was a great salesperson and a great sales manager. But his story was a painfully sad one and ended with a self-inflicted gunshot to his temple. He told me enough about his life that I can personally fill in a few of the puzzling pieces behind this extreme act.

Businesswise, he'd climbed to the top of his game. He was a highly successful manager of a life insurance agency in a very large city; he'd managed one of the top agencies of his whole company.

Two years earlier, after being certified to conduct my Managing Goal Achievement course for his own producers, he shared with me that his life had been in a slump for two or three years, and he was looking for this to pull him out.

Two months later, he sent me a picture of a large new home for which he set a goal to build. He told me how excited he was for his family, and asked me if I'd be the first person to have dinner in his new home when it was finished.

In the next few months, his business went through the roof. He was a rising star in his company. Each month he sent me his agency's sales production figures, as well as his standing among the other agencies in his company.

It had taken five to six years for me to get to know him. At first, he always seemed removed and aloof. After a few years, he began calling me to visit with me, both over the phone and in person. Three times in the year before his death, he came to Phoenix to visit me. In small increments, he told me a strange story about the family in which he grew up. His father, a Jewish immigrant, was a rag and junk collector when my friend was a boy. He told me of the embarrassment he felt when his friends saw him riding with his dad in an old dilapidated truck, picking up junk.

He told me the following story four or five times. When he was in high school and he and his dad were out collecting junk, his father pulled the truck up to the front of a malt shop where students at his school gathered. His dad handed him some money and told him to go in and get them each a malt. Slumping down in the truck so his friends couldn't see him, he refused. His father said, "Okay," and went into the shop and came out with a malt for himself but not one for my friend.

Back in the truck, while enjoying his own malt, his father gave him a very stern lecture about his behavior. The incident obviously burned a deep impression on my friend.

He told me that he always deeply felt that his father did not approve of his success. He secretly wanted to be highly successful to please his father. But it seemed the harder he tried and the more successful he became, the more disapproval he received. And I suspect, the more disapproval he received the harder he tried to be successful.

Apparently there were many incidents of his father controlling him with negative responses. He told me another story several times. After he was grown and earning a very nice income, he bought a lifelong dream car—a Porsche. He then called his father to tell him what he had, hoping, I'm sure, that he would receive his father's approval for being so successful. He had to explain to his father what a Porsche was. His father exploded when he heard the news and told him that he didn't deserve to have a car like that and that he shouldn't keep it and should take it back.

My friend told me of the anger and the deep emotional hurt he experienced after the phone call. Rather than feeling a sense of accomplishment, he was shattered. As he told me this story, he looked at me with incredible pain in his eyes and said, "And . . . I took it back." Slowly he went on, "There was something within me that I couldn't seem to control. Ever since then I've always dreamed of having another one, but even though I can afford one, I could never bring myself to buy one."

As we had agreed months earlier, I was the first dinner guest in his new home—two days after his family moved in. Everyone seemed so happy.

It was only a very short time later that I got the call. They found him in the men's room of an adjoining office building. He had shot himself.

No note. No explanation. Nothing in his pockets except a business card.

No one has the faintest logical idea why he did it.

I can only offer a slightly enlightened guess. The more his success increased, the greater his internal conflict grew. His high degree of success could well have been driven by his deep need to please his father, and prove his worth to others; but paradoxically, the more success he enjoyed the more intensely he felt out of synch with his deep, well-set inner programming.

Maybe it was the programming of poverty in his "I Am" that interacted with his actual achievements and was carried out by his "I Think" that created such incredible conflicts for him. So he could no longer deal with the internal pain of them. No one who knew him had any inkling of the demons he struggled with. My guess is that the die had been unconsciously cast years before.

I miss him. We were friends.

Emotions Are More Powerful Than Logic

After observing thousands of people, I believe that, all things being equal, if we analyze a cross section of people we'll find they are moti-

vated about 85 percent by feelings and emotions, and about 15 percent
by logic. This is important to emphasize as we think of goal achievement,
because the latter has little to do with logic or process. It has everything
to do with who we internally believe we are, and what we unconsciously
think we deserve to have. These feelings of worthiness or unworthiness
will cause deep emotional reactions to goals we set, and either allow
them to happen or prevent that.

A Spiritual Journey

Since the "I Am" part of us is the spiritual dimension, then the journey
of wholeness, completeness, and soundness must by its nature be a spiritual walk. It's in the merging with the Infinite that the simplicity and the
complexity of all human journeys lie.

Herein lies the secret of proper care and feeding of our spiritual
natures—that we learn to love. Scott Peck defines love as "the will to
extend one's self for the purpose of nurturing one's own or another's
spiritual growth."

It is in seeking the highest good for ourselves and others that we
love. Whenever we do this, we nurture our spiritual selves. These paradoxical moments, then, become the ones in which we feel most alive,
and build our "I Am" dimensions.

Conventional wisdom tells us that success, self-fulfillment, and prosperity are achieved in the acts of *getting*. Spiritual discernment tells us
that true peace of mind and prosperity consciousness result from what
we *give*. Does this mean that it's wrong to set prosperity goals? No,
absolutely not, as long as we understand that true prosperity is the over-
flow we enjoy for the value we create in life. It can come in many
forms—money, recognition, appreciation, self-respect, or feeling good
about ourselves because of what we contribute to others.

The paradox is that we internally feel better about ourselves more
because of what we contribute than what we receive, although in the
scheme of things we must freely receive if we have freely given. So it
comes down to our choices. What we logically think will make us happy,
often doesn't, and what we may not think will bring us fulfillment, often
does. Human wisdom and spiritual discernment are often at odds.

Congruent Values, Beliefs, and Goals

Are your inner values and beliefs congruent with your goals? That's a key question. It gets right to the real issue. Conflicts between your values and goals block your achievement. They stress and confuse you. They create a dissonance in your "I Am."

Here's a series of questions that can help you understand more of the complexities of goal achievement.

1. *What goals have I set, only to discover that I never really thought that I could reach them?*
2. *What goals have I set, only to realize they were in conflict with my values or other goals?*
3. *Have I set goals that were in conflict with what people around me wanted me to reach?*
4. *Who do I have in my life whose self-perceived role is to torpedo my goal achievement?*
5. *Who do I have in my life who positively supports my goal achievement?*
6. *Does the thought of setting new goals cause me to get excited, or does it elicit memories of past failures in my mind?*
7. *Could I be reluctant to commit to goals because I don't want to set up more possible failures?*
8. *Does the thought of reaching new goals cause me to ask, "What could go wrong?" or "What could go right?"? Do I focus on the difficulties or the rewards of reaching my goals?* (One weakens you; the other strengthens you.)
9. *What goals are possible for me to attain, given my role in life at this time?*
10. *What are some life experiences I've had that helped program my "I Am" to have the beliefs it currently holds?*

As you sincerely ask yourself these questions, you'll begin to develop some insights into your unconscious beliefs about what's possible for you to attain. In time, the truth will emerge.

HOW TO GAIN THE MOST FROM THIS CHAPTER

Consider what Maltz wrote about your inner mechanism in *Psycho-Cybernetics*:

> Every living thing has a built-in guidance system or goal-striving device, put there by its Creator to help it achieve its goal—which is, in broad terms—to live.

This Creative Mechanism is so powerful that it taps into the most dynamic forces deep within you. When this mechanism is focused toward worthwhile goals that are consistent with your views of your *possibilities,* your *values,* and *beliefs* about *who* you are and *what* you deserve to enjoy in life, it's released to seek out ways for you to attain them. It feeds you hunches, insights, and ideas and opens doors previously closed. It helps you recognize resources you haven't discovered before.

Reflect on your life and see if you can think of times when your prevailing, dominant desires, whether negative or positive, became goals, and your Goal-Seeking Mechanism silently steered you toward them.

Fear, anxiety, worry, or doubting are to be understood and replaced with positive, prosperity-oriented thoughts.

As you go about your week, consider the following:

1. Observe high-producing salespeople and discover the creative ideas they use.
2. Ask yourself each day, "What can I do that they do that will help me reach higher sales goals?"
3. Examine your current goals and listen for hunches, or insights on how to reach them.
4. Carefully choose thoughts and self-talk that are positive.

And in your off moments this week, feed your mind with this self-talk: "I focus daily on what I want to happen in my life, and not on what I don't want to happen."

6 DISCOVERING YOUR CREATIVE GOAL-SEEKING
MECHANISM

Assessment

Take a few moments and check off the number that best describes your present beliefs, boundaries, or behaviors. Use these descriptors as guidelines.

5–Always true, without exception
4–Mostly true
3–True more often than not
2–True only part of the time
1–True only occasionally

Left	5 4 3 2 1	1 2 3 4 5	Right
1. I just stick to the old way of selling.	5 4 3 2 1	1 2 3 4 5	1. I constantly look for creative ways to better serve my clients.
2. I'm so busy trying to make a living that I never can look beyond that.	5 4 3 2 1	1 2 3 4 5	2. I'm always challenging my old beliefs about what's possible for me to sell.
3. I think more about my problems than my possibilities.	5 4 3 2 1	1 2 3 4 5	3. I talk more about my possibilities than my problems.
4. I talk in terms of "what has been."	5 4 3 2 1	1 2 3 4 5	4. I think in terms of "what can be."
5. I think visualizing how I can do better is a waste of time.	5 4 3 2 1	1 2 3 4 5	5. I spend time daily visualizing how I can do things better.
6. Once I realize that I'm not going to reach a goal, I abandon it.	5 4 3 2 1	1 2 3 4 5	6. I continually revise my goals.
7. I don't know what "hunches" and "intuition" are.	5 4 3 2 1	1 2 3 4 5	7. I listen to my hunches and intuition about my improvement.
8. Setting goals seems to disturb me and stress me out.	5 4 3 2 1	1 2 3 4 5	8. I experience no inner conflicts about my goals.

	5 4 3 2 1	1 2 3 4 5	
9. When I set a goal I spend most of my time worrying about whether or not it will happen.	5 4 3 2 1	1 2 3 4 5	9. When I set a goal I spend most of my time planning how to make it happen.
10. I have no idea of how to reach higher goals than I'm now reaching.	5 4 3 2 1	1 2 3 4 5	10. I always assume that higher goals are possible, and I can find the way to reach them.

- Add up the numbers in the right-hand column. _____
- Add up the numbers in the left-hand column. _____
- Subtract the left-hand column total from the right-hand column total and score yourself. _____

Assessments scoring guide is on page 35.

Keeping Score—Chapter 6

Behavior that gets evaluated, gets improved.

On a scale of 1–10, please evaluate your performance of each of these Action Guides.

	S	M	T	W	T	F	S
1. I have written new goals, and I reviewed them today.							
2. I asked myself, "What can I do that successful people do that will help me reach my goals?" several times today.							
3. I took a few minutes, cut out my world and examined my self-beliefs, and opened my mind to receive hunches and insights about how to reach my goals.							
4. I carefully chose positive thoughts and self-talk to focus on.							
Total Each Day							

7 Customer Focus
How to Sell the Way Customers Want to Buy

MIKE DICKENSHIED OF MARKQUART TOYOTA IN EAU CLAIRE, Wisconsin, shared a great example of customer needs–focused selling.

A young person came into his dealership to look for a vehicle. "She didn't look like the type anyone would take seriously," he began. "After introducing myself, getting her name, and briefly discussing what she was interested in, we came into my office and sat down. I asked her several questions about what was important to her in her choice of vehicles. She began talking and I just listened.

"This was not the first dealership she had visited. I could tell she wasn't happy with the other places. I found out quickly that they hadn't listened to her, and had dismissed her as someone who couldn't afford to buy a car. I helped her find a vehicle that she liked and could afford, and she is now driving it."

"I listened to her where I don't believe other dealers did. I learned that I can sell more by listening to people than by trying to talk them into buying."

Great lesson, and a great choice in a way to professionally sell.

Each day all salespeople make a fundamental decision. They decide to sell the way:

1. They want their customers to buy, or
2. The way their customers themselves want to buy.

Think about it for a moment. What's your intent or objective when you contact customers, clients, members, patients, or guests? Is your purpose to try to get them to buy from you? Is it to sell them something? To do something *to* them? Or to do something *for* them?

There are basically three selling strategies: *product-focused, transaction-focused,* or *customer needs–focused.*

Product-focused is where you flood your prospective customers with loads of information about your product or service. You tell them all about the features, benefits, and advantages of whatever you're selling. You dominate most of the conversation, and eventually you ask them to buy it.

Your assumption is that something you say will hit their "hot button" and they'll come alive and say, "Yes, that's what I need. How much will it cost me?"

Try to buy a new car and see if the salesman doesn't tell you about features that you have no interest in knowing about. He'll talk to you about the new electronic ignition system, or how the cam shaft is manufactured, what size the wheel bearings are, and all you want to know is, "How fast will it go, and can I get it in red?"

Wouldn't it be nice if he'd first found out what you were interested in and then focused on explaining that?

Because of their excitement about their own product features, salespeople often forget that customers buy products or services for what they will do for them, not for what they are. People don't usually buy products or services just to have them; they buy to enjoy end-result benefits or rewards they'll receive.

Transaction-focused describes more of a commodity purchase, where the features and benefits are pretty much known, and a salesperson is simply attempting to close a sale, often based on price.

Take the salesperson who called me recently wanting to sell me gold coins. Or the stock broker who recommends a particular stock to a client. Or the wholesaler who's attempting to sell a carload of soap.

Customer needs–focused follows a different path than the others. Your first objective is to gain rapport with potential customers. You put them at ease, break your own preoccupation, tune your world out, and put your attention on them.

You approach people with a totally different mind-set than you do in product- or transaction-focused selling. You approach them with the attitude: "I'm not just trying to sell you something; rather, I want to find out if you have needs or wants I can satisfy for you." Or, "If you have problems, I can help you solve them. Or, "There are goals I can help you reach."

See the difference? It's huge!

This way you're selling solutions, while other salespeople are still trying to sell products or services.

You don't even talk about your product until someone says, "Yes, I have a want, need, problem, or goal that I want help reaching or satisfying." Only when you feel your solution is appropriate for them do you tell them how your product will give them the satisfaction, fulfillment, or benefits they want.

In a real sense, you're not selling products or services, you're selling solutions, gratification, rewards, enjoyment. End-result benefits.

How Do Customers Want to Buy?

Let's put this question in the proper perspective. It's not *how do you want to sell*. It's *how do your customers want to buy*.

Examine your own purchases. Who do you constantly enjoy buying things from? Why do you enjoy it? What do they do to cause you to continue your relationship with them? Do you like to buy from them because they put pressure on you? Or because they're only interested in what they can sell you?

Probably not. I've learned that salespeople who try to pressure people to buy from them don't want to be sold to themselves that way.

I remember calling on a car dealer several years ago. His dealership was widely known for being manipulative and "slam dunk" in their sales approaches with customers. He was hard as nails, and when I shared with him the results we had achieved with other dealers, he asked how we did it. I explained our Integrity Selling needs-based selling process, and how it was the opposite of "high-pressure" selling. As I explained this to him, he became very red in the face and almost attacked me.

He dismissed me quickly, accusing me of using "high pressure" tactics on him, which in no way described my conversation with him.

The humor and the irony of the call kept me shaking my head and laughing at the experience. It did make a good point, though. People may try to put pressure on others, but they don't want others doing it to them.

Integrity Selling

Our Integrity Selling course is a complete process of selling to people the way they want to buy. And the fact is that when salespeople follow our process, they almost always sell more—no matter what they're selling.

Aim Funds in Houston, Texas, for example, told us that for every one dollar they invested with us they enjoyed $352 in new sales. Trade New Zealand reported an increase of $500 million in trade after training their people with Integrity Selling. The North Atlantic Region of American Red Cross reported a 35 percent increase in blood sales, and a 50 percent reduction in employee turnover.

A large division of Johnson & Johnson reported a 26 percent sales increase in Japan, 28 percent in South Africa. Coldwell Banker agents in Florida reported an average 25 percent increase in sales.

In a pilot, twelve Chevrolet dealers averaged reporting a 25 percent increase in closing ratios and 31 percent increase in gross margins per sale.

The Integrity Selling System has six steps. They are:

1. Approach—to gain rapport
2. Interview—to identify and get agreement of needs
3. Demonstrate—to explain how features and benefits will satisfy their admitted needs
4. Validate—to prove your claims and develop trust
5. Negotiate—to work out problems that keep people from buying
6. Close—to ask for a decision at the right time

The AID, Inc. System

I call this the AID, Inc. System. To make it fit this acronym, we need to change the way we pronounce *validate* to *val-I-date*.

Notice the graphic representation of the system on page 142.

The AID, Inc. System

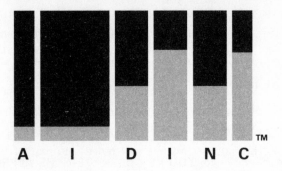

A   I   D   I   N   C

Going from left to right, you'll see the approximate percent of time that each step takes. Vertically, the lower shaded-in areas represent the approximate percent of time you spend talking, while the top part is the amount of time your customers talk, and you listen.

You'll notice that in the first two steps you do 20 percent of the talking and 80 percent of the listening. By observing the following three rules for using the process you have a complete system.

1. Always find out where you are with your customers and begin at that point.
2. Always complete one step before going to the next one.
3. Never jump to a step without completing the prior ones.

Let's take a quick trip through the process. For some of you this will be a review; others will learn it for the first time.

The Approach

The Approach is the first sale you should focus on completing. The sale you'll make is to get the person(s) you're contacting comfortable with you. To cut out their world and devote their attention span to you. To mentally and physically unfold their arms.

You'll want to carefully approach people whether it's the first or the fifty-first time you've contacted them.

Here are the Action Guides for the Approach step:

1. *Tune* the world out and people in.
2. *Put* them at ease and make them feel important.

3. *Get* them talking about themselves.

4. *Hold* eye contact and listen to how they feel.

Your sincere interest in your customers as people, along with your ability to ask them open-ended questions, will get them talking about subjects they're interested in. This will cause you to enjoy an effective approach. The secret is understanding what they want to talk about, and asking appropriate questions.

HOW TO KNOW WHEN YOU'VE COMPLETED THE APPROACH STEP

Here's a checklist to help you know when you've completed this first important step.

1. People seem comfortable and open up to you.
2. They appear ready to move on to share their needs with you.
3. They indicate that they have time to get into your interview.
4. You can get the necessary people together for a fact-finding interview.

Everyone you approach enjoys talking about themselves, their interests, reasons for their success, their family, their hobbies, their life story, or their current activities.

It's knowing the right questions to ask that helps you enjoy a successful approach.

Interview

The Interview is the heart of a customer needs–focused selling process. Your goal is to find out if a person has needs you can help them fill, and if they do, to understand what they are. You ask well-crafted, open-ended questions.

Think of the professionalism of a physician for a moment. When you go in to see her does she immediately begin to try to sell you a new procedure, or a new drug? No, she greets you, sits you down, and asks you questions, such as "Where does it hurt?" "How long has it been feeling this way?" "What are other symptoms?" She may do tests, or find out other information, but her objective is to find out what your problem is so she can prescribe a cure—if indeed she can.

You'd be skeptical of her professionalism if she immediately began telling you about a new drug on the market and then asked you to buy it.

Take the same model and apply it to your selling role.

This professional process can be duplicated by you when you discover the power of the Interview step. Here are the Interview Action Guides.

1. *Ask* open-ended, indirect questions that draw out wants or needs.
2. *Listen* to and paraphrase all points—write them down.
3. *Identify* dominant wants or needs and get agreement.
4. *Assure* people that you want to help them enjoy the most value.

The effectiveness of your Interview increases as you embrace these attitudes.

1. "I'm not here to sell you something, I'm here to understand if you have wants, needs, problems, challenges, or goals for which I can provide you with solutions."
2. "I'm not sure my product or service is right for you, and wouldn't know until I understand your needs."
3. "I'd like to ask you some questions that will give me information so I can understand what you want to achieve."
4. "I will not attempt to sell you anything unless it will best fill your needs, and offer you the best solutions."
5. "I am really selling solutions rather than products or services."

As you gain their permission you should ask questions that contain the "six honest serving men" that Rudyard Kipling wrote about. They are *who, what, where, why, when, how.* Ask these questions in a fact-finding way, not in a leading manner. Your whole objective at this point is to get information that helps you understand their wants or needs.

Once you understand people's needs, and if your product will provide an excellent solution, you'll then go to the Demonstration or presentation step.

HOW TO KNOW WHEN YOU'VE COMPLETED THE INTERVIEW STEP

1. People admit a want or need that they want filled or satisfied.
2. They're willing to talk to you about a solution.

3. You've gathered enough information to recommend a solution.
4. You've identified the decision makers.

Demonstration

This is your show-and-tell presentation step, where you share how your product or service will fill the admitted needs of your customer.

In the ideal world this is the first you've talked about your solutions—whether they be products or services. In this context you're only talking about how your product or service will provide your customers with the solutions they admitted wanting.

See how everything evolves around your customers' admitted needs? The Demonstrate Action Guides are:

1. *Repeat* the dominant wants or needs that have been admitted.
2. *Show* or tell how your product or service will fill their wants or needs.
3. *Avoid* talking about price. Make it secondary to finding out what best fills their needs.
4. *Ask* for their reactions, feelings, or opinions.

It's in this step that you present the price of your recommendation. You'll always be careful to present it at the right time. The right time is when people fully understand your product's features and benefits and how they'll fill their needs.

Until people want the solution your product will give them, price is irrelevant. If they don't understand or want it, it makes no difference what the price is. We have a saying, "Never quote price to an unsold buyer."

This is the crucial point when customers must be convinced that their needs will be filled, and what you're selling is worth more to them than the money they'll pay you for it. Here's where you want to know the *truth* and the truth is whatever they're thinking. Before going on with your sales efforts, you should make sure customers believe the value outweighs the price.

HOW TO KNOW WHEN YOU'VE COMPLETED THE DEMONSTRATION STEP
1. People understand your recommendation and believe it will fill their wants or needs.

2. Their questions and concerns have been successfully answered.
3. Everyone who has decision influence has been included in your presentation.
4. You've identified any roadblocks, concerns, or apprehensions they may have had about making a decision.

Conducting your approach, interview and demonstration as I've outlined here helps you to be customer needs–focused and not product- or transaction-focused.

Val-I-date

You'll commonly need to validate yourself, your product, service, or organization as ones of integrity. People are often silently asking: "Can I trust you? Your product? Your organization?"

Validation isn't necessarily a separate step of AID, Inc. Actually, it's an ongoing process. You do it from start to finish to follow-up. The reason why it's placed where it is is that you must validate at this point if you're going to make the sale.

The Val-I-date Action Guides are as follows:

1. *Translate* product or service features into customer benefits.
2. *Justify* price and emphasize value.
3. *Offer* proof and evidence.
4. *Reassure* and reinforce people to neutralize their fear of buying.

When you're validating your offering, you'll want to remember what your customers' wants or needs are, and identify the inner motive that's causing them to buy. Let me explain that people don't buy products or services; they buy *perceived value*. This fact makes it essential for you to know what their real reason for buying is.

Different people buy for different reasons. People who purchase things always have a dominant buying motive—a main reason for buying something.

Notice the model on page 147. It shows how people make purchase decisions.

Before you check off that you've completed the Validation step, you

The Perceived Value Process:
The Customer's Viewpoint

- How I'll look

- How I'll feel

- What I'll enjoy

- How I'll be protected

- How others will think of me $\quad\Big\}\quad \div$ Price = Perceived Value

- How long it'll last

- How proud I'll be of it

- How much I need it

- How badly I want it

should have a good idea about what your customer's *perceived value* needs are. Of course, this is part of your interview.

To identify people's perceived value you must use your intuition and go deeper with your questions. You must keep thinking and asking, "What other concerns or issues do I need to understand?" "What will be the rewards of having this product or service?"

HOW TO KNOW WHEN YOU'VE COMPLETED THE VALIDATION STEP

1. People seem to trust you and believe your claims.
2. They are convinced of the efficacy of your product or service.
3. They believe that your organization will stand behind your product or service performance.
4. They respect you for your integrity.

Negotiation

The Negotiation step is often misunderstood. Many people have attended seminars, read books, or heard speakers present negotiation as a strategy to convince people to change their minds. To see things from the salesperson's perspective. For customers to see the error of their own thinking. Many people also see it as a process of mentally outmaneuvering others.

Cute, funny war stories can be shared about how a slick salesman put it over an intelligence-challenged prospect. But who of us wants this done to us?

In Integrity Selling we describe Negotiation as a process of working out problems that keep people from buying . . . when they want to work out the problems and buy from us.

See the difference? There's no confrontation.

Here are the Negotiation Action Guides:

1. *Find* out what concerns or objections remain.
2. *Welcome* and understand objections.
3. *Identify* and isolate specific objections.
4. *Discuss* possible solutions—ask their opinions for best solutions.

When we do a great job of interviewing, we usually find out what possible objections might arise—before they come up. So when we get to the Negotiation phase, we've already dealt with them.

When objections do arise, you'll want to ask your customers some questions such as:

- *Would you explain your concern to me so I understand it?*
- *Is the solution I offered worth more to you than the cost or time spent working out this problem?*
- *What are your suggestions about how we work through this concern?*
- *Who can we bring in to help us work through this challenge?*

I always like to remember the clarification question: "Is the pain of your problem greater than the cost of the cure?" Of course, you can phrase this question several ways.

Effective negotiation is like sitting down on the same side of the table with someone, and asking, "Is this a problem that you want to work out?" When people say, "Yes, I want what your offering me, but I have a challenge to work out," you then team up with them and work through their concern or problem.

HOW TO KNOW WHEN YOU'VE COMPLETED THE NEGOTIATION STEP
You'll know you've completed the Negotiation step when:

1. People want your product or service if their concerns can be worked through.
2. You've identified their concerns or objections.
3. You understand what each person wants from the transaction.
4. You've successfully worked through all their concerns or objections.

Close

Closing is simply asking for a decision at the right time. So, when *is* the right time to ask? It's when your customer is ready to say, "Yes."

Your customer is only ready to say "Yes" when you've successfully:

- *Approached* and gained rapport.
- *Identified* and agreed upon real wants or needs.
- *Demonstrated* a solution that your customers believe will satisfy their needs.
- *Validated* to cause your customers to believe, trust, and have confidence in you.
- *Negotiated* to work out the problems that would keep them from buying.

When you've completed all of these five steps, what's left but to ask for a decision?

These are the Close Action Guides:

1. *Ask* trial-closing questions to get opinions and responses.
2. *Listen* to and reinforce each response.
3. *Restate* how the benefits will outweigh the costs.
4. *Ask* for a decision.

Let me emphasize that *trial-closing questions* are ones you ask to get opinions; closing questions are ones you ask to get decisions.

Opinion questions typically include:

- *What other questions or concerns do you have that we need to discuss before making a decision?*
- *At this point, what have I failed to explain?*

- *Who might have some decision input that we haven't gotten agreement from?*
- *At this point, do you clearly see how the benefits of my solution outweigh the costs to you?*
- *Would you explain your decision process or criteria again?*
- *At this point, do you need more validation or evidence of the benefits I can give you?*

Trial-closing questions call for explanations; closing questions call for "yes" or "no" answers.

Before you ever ask a closing question you should be convinced yourself that your product or service will give your customers the end-result benefits they want. You're operating with integrity when you wouldn't sell something to people unless it best fills their needs and creates value for them above the price they pay you for it.

Closing isn't just about *you* winning, it's about both you *and* your customer winning.

HOW TO KNOW WHEN YOU'VE COMPLETED THE CLOSE STEP

1. Everyone's concerns have been successfully worked through.
2. They understand how the benefits of your product or service will exceed their cost.
3. They want what you have.
4. They're ready to take the appropriate closing action.

So, here you have the six AID, Inc. steps. Whether you're an entry-level salesperson or a highly successful veteran, you can use this process to help you serve your customers most effectively. And serving your customers most appropriately is the best way to build your own career success.

AID, Inc. Is the How You Sell

We have people all over the world using the Integrity Selling, AID, Inc. system. People just starting out find it very helpful; veterans earning over $1 million a year tell me that they continue to find it challenging.

I developed the system over two decades ago, and I've never mastered it. I've never done as good an Interview as I'd like to do. The reason is that every person and selling situation has different needs, wants, solutions, and goals. Finding out people's real buying motives requires finesse, skills, and wisdom. Understanding people's many hidden agendas is a never-ending challenge.

HOW TO GAIN THE MOST FROM THIS CHAPTER

Review the AID, Inc. steps often, follow the Action Guides, and evaluate your performance against the four ways to know when you've completed each step.

Check yourself on how much time you spend talking in each step, and how much time listening. Think through your different questions—when you Approach, Interview, Demonstrate, Val-I-date, Negotiate, and Close.

Remember the rules for using the AID, Inc. process.

1. Always find out where you are with your customers and begin at that point.
2. Always complete the step before going to the next one.
3. Never jump to a step before completing the ones before it.

So there you have it: a complete system that can be the foundation for a highly successful sales career. The thing to do now is practice, practice, practice.

You can take advantage of moments when you're waiting for a red light to change or for an appointment; feed your mind this positive self-suggestion: "When I give customers more value than they expect, I receive more rewards than I expect."

7 HOW TO SELL THE WAY CUSTOMERS WANT TO BUY

Assessment

Please take a few moments and check off the number that best describes your true, present beliefs, boundaries, or behaviors. Use these descriptors as guidelines.

> 5–Always true, without exception
> 4–Mostly true
> 3–True more often than not
> 2–True only part of the time
> 1–True only occasionally

1. I view selling as getting customers to do something for me.	5 4 3 2 1 | 1 2 3 4 5	1. I view selling as doing something for customers.
2. I view what I do as selling products or services.	5 4 3 2 1 | 1 2 3 4 5	2. I view what I do as identifying and satisfying customers' needs.
3. I get down to business immediately.	5 4 3 2 1 | 1 2 3 4 5	3. I always spend the first few minutes gaining rapport with customers.
4. I usually do most of the talking during the first part of contact.	5 4 3 2 1 | 1 2 3 4 5	4. I do about 20 percent of the talking in the first part of a contact.
5. I always jump into a product explanation soon after contacting customers.	5 4 3 2 1 | 1 2 3 4 5	5. I never talk about my products until customers admit a need for what I have.
6. I focus mostly on stressing my product features, hoping I say something that causes customers to want it.	5 4 3 2 1 | 1 2 3 4 5	6. I carefully fit my product features to customers' admitted needs.

	5 4 3 2 1	1 2 3 4 5	
7. I never ask response questions when I'm explaining my product. I don't want to lose control.	5 4 3 2 1	1 2 3 4 5	7. I ask demonstrative response questions so I know what my customers' feelings are.
8. When I meet objections I always try to overcome them and convince customers to see things my way.	5 4 3 2 1	1 2 3 4 5	8. Before discussing customers' concerns, I always make sure they want what I'm offering.
9. My own needs to make a sale always drive me to close hard.	5 4 3 2 1	1 2 3 4 5	9. I always make sure that what I'm offering is the best solution for my customers.
10. I have so much pressure on me that I don't have time to develop relationships with customers.	5 4 3 2 1	1 2 3 4 5	10. Developing trust and rapport is more important to me than making a quick sale.

- Add up the numbers in the right-hand column. _____
- Add up the numbers in the left-hand column. _____
- Subtract the left-hand column total from the right-hand column total and score yourself. _____

Assessments scoring guide is on page 35.

Keeping Score—Chapter 7

Behavior that gets evaluated, gets improved.

On a scale of 1–10, please evaluate your performance of each of these parts of the Breakthrough Process.

	S	M	T	W	T	F	S
1. I reviewed and applied the *Approach* Action Guides today.							
2. I followed the *Interview* Action Guides today.							
3. I applied the *Demonstrate* Action Guides today.							
4. I applied the *Validate* Action Guides today.							
5. I applied the *Negotiate* Action Guides today.							
6. I applied the *Close* Action Guides today.							
Total Each Day							

8 Energy
Releasing Unlimited Achievement Drive

WHEN YOU THINK ABOUT OUTSTANDING SALESPEOPLE, Thomas Edison may not be the first person to pop into your mind. A great inventor? Yes. A great salesman? Well!

The truth is that he had to sell everything he invented. From the phonograph, which he sold in 1877 as a music player and office dictating machine, to the electric light bulb, which he initially sold to two hundred companies across America, everything had to be sold.

It was a combination of stubborn tenacity and an incredibly strong achievement drive that motivated him. Just think what he started with—little or no formal education, constant resistance, scores of people attempting to steal his patents. It was his indomitable will to succeed that brought light, sound, and pictures to the world.

Edison's work ethic was legendary. Working around the clock for days in a row with only short naps to keep him going, he was a driven man. What drove him to such energy, we can only speculate. Certainly few people ever started with less.

Yet his internal drive to succeed produced results that had never been seen before.

What was it that helped him release this kind of energy? To achieve what no person had ever achieved before? Where did he ever get the vision or belief that what he eventually did could even be done?

The Human Quest for Achievement

There appears to be latent within people an inexhaustible potential creative power. Tragically, most people go through life never accessing it.

Harvard's David McClelland coined the terms *achievement drive* and *n-achievement,* or "need for achievement." He studied individuals, organizations, and nations and theorized that those that exhibit high need for achievement tend to excel despite lack of knowledge, natural resources, or other limiting factors.

The need to achieve is a restlessness within people that motivates them to learn, acquire skills, and take risks.

McClelland believed that achievement drive is the multiplying factor in our success. It doesn't just add to our other skills and abilities, it actually multiplies them. This is important to keep remembering—especially in a world where knowledge is thought to be power. Tragically, our formal education system doesn't recognize this.

The Multiplying Factor in Selling

Achievement drive is spawned by your inner need to succeed; your belief that you can enjoy high rewards; that being successful is consistent with who you are.

As you did in Chapter 4, take a moment and on a scale of 1–10 assess yourself for the following factors. Then add up the first five and multiply them times your achievement drive rating. This gives you your sales power.

	Knowledge	_____
+	Sales Skills	_____
+	Inherent Abilities	_____
+	Selling Experience	_____
+	Products and Resources	_____
×	Achievement Drive	_____
=	Sales Power	_____

Your need for achievement acts as a catalyst in creating energy that then shows up in behaviors like persistence, determination, good time management, and openness to learn.

Now that a few weeks have gone by, stop and score yourself in this formula. On a scale of 1–10, evaluate each trait, experience, or product competitive value. Add up the first five scores, get a total, and then multiply it times your achievement score. This gives you your sales power quotient. Your highest possible score is 500.

For the sake of comparison, let's assume that a person has high skills but low drive. Let's say his total of the first five traits is a high 40. Since this person has low drive, let's give him a 2. His sales power would be 80.

Not very good, is it?

But you all know people who fit this profile, don't you?

On the other hand, consider a person with lower skills or traits, but who has high drive. Let's score him a 5 on each of the first five traits, for a total of 25. Multiply this times a high achievement drive score of 9 and you have someone with a total score of 225.

The reality is that a person with high drive will quickly learn what she needs to know to achieve higher goals. So these lower skill or trait numbers will soon rise because the person sees it is necessary to acquire them in order to reach her goals.

Hot Beliefs

Years ago, Harvard professor William James, writing about human behavior, used the term *hot beliefs* to describe the intensity of inner beliefs that motivate people to action.

He wrote, "Hot beliefs have a motor effect." In simple terms, they always lead us to action. It's getting excited, passionate, or pumped up about the possibilities of our goals happening, and then taking action. The degree of intensity predicts the level of achievement drive that will be released from within us. The level of drive then motivates the energy of our actions.

James pointed out that hot beliefs bring about changes in behaviors and performance. He also wrote that when "cold beliefs," those without passion or belief, become "hot," not only new energies, but a new level of willpower and apparent abilities seem to be released.

Here's where we make big mistakes in attempting to motivate ourselves. Trying to reach goals with muscled-up willpower or self-discipline usually doesn't take us too far. Achievement drive is not released by willpower. Attempting to do it creates frustration, burnout, and, eventually, failed performance.

I've seen salesperson after salesperson fail when they were managed by activities. A manager's ultimatum, "Give me so many calls each week," usually predicts low performance.

Logic rarely releases achievement drive, because our emotions aren't under the direct control of our rational processes. Emotions are released from desire, belief, need for recognition, and other deep drives that we'll consider in this chapter.

Traits of High Achievers

Your need to achieve is driven by deep values, beliefs, and desires that inhabit your "I Am." Usually these are the result of your upbringing, parents, or key life influences. Many people are highly motivated to achieve because their parents always told them they could do anything they set out to do. Others come from the opposite kind of influence where their parents were low achievers, and this motivated them to accomplish great things.

Many high achievers act out of a personal need for recognition. Others have a sincere need to serve others. Some people want to perform at high levels to impress others. Others want to give to worthy causes anonymously since they have no need for public recognition. A person's values enter the mix.

High achievement drive exhibits itself in people who are willing to take calculated risks. They set challenging yet achievable goals. They usually show a single-minded passion for their chosen field. They're motivated to learn—not just for the sake of knowledge, but for the practical aspects that will help them reach their individual goals.

Salespeople with high achievement drive tend to read more self-help books, listen to audio messages, and attend events where other high achievers go. They seek out and learn from other successful people.

Along with his scientific research, McClelland devised a simple way of predicting achievement drive levels within people. He got a group of people together and put before them a child's ring-toss game, the kind with a peg that holds several round rope rings. The goal is to toss the ring onto the peg. He watched the people play with it, and made an interesting observation.

People who were overly careful placed the peg so close in that they could hardly miss. To McClelland this showed they had a very low risk tolerance, which translated into a high need for security and predictability, and low need to win or beat other people.

One group placed the peg at distances that made it very difficult to actually toss a peg on it. In doing this, they set unrealistic goals and always had an excuse for not scoring.

The third group carefully calculated how far out to place the peg so it gave them a challenge, but a manageable one. They seemed to unconsciously position the peg so that they had almost a 50 percent chance of throwing the ring over it.

In a sense they wanted to take "manageable risks." They desired a challenge, but one that gave them a reasonable chance of success. They seemed to intuitively know how to stretch themselves but still remain within attainable odds of success.

High achievers also know that they'll not always reach their challenging goals. They want a high hit rate, but know it will not be 100 percent. They can emotionally handle that.

In short, they want challenge, but also want to ensure a reasonable chance for success. Interestingly enough, McClelland found this game to be a highly predictive way to measure people's achievement drive.

Achievement Drive Can Be Unlocked

Since everyone has the latent potential to release this energy, we should look at it, not as something externally poured into us, but as *internally* released.

Understanding this, the question becomes, "How is it released?"

Again, we have to look inward rather than at external circumstances. We must understand that it's a matter of certain internal factors coming together. Let's take a deeper look at the Goal Achievement Congruence Model that I introduced earlier (see page 160).

Goal Achievement
Congruence Model

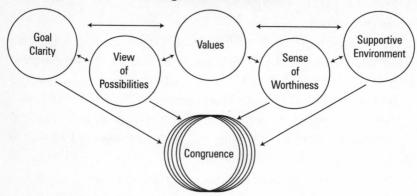

Here's an explanation of the five different dimensions.

1. Goal Clarity—having clear, specific, written goals of what you want to happen in your future
2. View of Possibilities—believing that your goals are possible for you to attain with reasonable effort
3. Values—the spiritual, moral, and ethical beliefs that guide your behaviors
4. Sense of Worthiness—possessing a deep feeling that you're worthy of higher goal achievement
5. Supportive Environment—being surrounded with people, places, and things that support and encourage higher goal achievement.

As these dimensions come into congruence within you, you'll naturally release more achievement drive. The release of energy is the effect, and the congruence of these dimensions is the cause. When you work on the cause, the resulting effect begins to happen almost mysteriously.

To the extent that gaps occur between these dimensions, conflicts, internal stress, and goal diffusion will occur.

The following actions will help you rev up your emotional engine and generate power by bringing these dimensions into congruence. Let's think of each of the five dimensions.

Goal Clarity

Go back to the goals you set in Chapter 5, bearing in mind my directions for managing your progress. As you review your goals, ask yourself, "Where am I with this goal—what is my progress?" "Are all my goals still important to me?" "How can I best use my time?" "What subgoals should I reach to take me to my main goal?"

As you reflect on these questions, you'll know whether to proceed, correct you course, or recycle.

Chances are if you're like most of us, after thinking about your goals for a week or so you'll probably want to revise some or all of them. This shows progress.

Look at your goals as ones you thought you wanted when you set them; however, after reflection you may find that you need to adjust them. Also, I recommend that you keep most of your goals just a bit beyond your current reach, so they're not so far in the distance that they lose their emotional pull. Often, the further your goals are the less you tend to believe in their possibilities, and the less their gratification seems imminent.

View of Possibilities

I've stressed repeatedly in this book the importance of building internal beliefs, or developing pictures of what you want to have, gain, possess, or achieve. Until we internally believe our goals to be possible, we'll exert little energy or drive to attain them. The truth is that more often than not, a goal is only an intangible idea when we set it, and is probably outside our current "area-of-the-possible."

Here are the specific actions that will help you strengthen your view of your possibilities.

1. Think of a similar goal you achieved sometime in the past. Say to yourself, "If I reached that goal (name it), I can reach this one (name it)."
2. Think of a person with education, skills, and training much as your own, who has reached similar-size goals you've just set. Think, "If (name) can reach goals like this, so can I."

3. Study, listen, and learn how other people who've reached goals you'd like to reach achieved them.
4. Review again Chapter 5, and study the Goal Achievement System.
5. Associate with people who are reaching goals you'd like to achieve.
6. Plan your strategy—designing a logical sequence of steps that will take you to your goals.

Values

Do a values check. Identify how reaching the new goals is indeed consistent with your real, internal values. Visualize how you'll feel healthy, happy, and fulfilled.

Here are six values that I've found help form a solid foundation for salespeople. Ask yourself, "Are my goals consistent with these statements?"

1. *I go the extra mile and give customers more than they expect to get.*
2. *I do the right thing because it's the right thing to do.*
3. *I focus on understanding and filling the wants or needs of others, knowing that when I do, my needs will be well filled.*
4. *I tell the truth in all situations, unless it would hurt someone.*
5. *I do unto others as I would have them do unto me.*
6. *I know I'll enjoy high levels of prosperity if I create high levels of value for others.*

Are your new goals consistent with your true values? Asked another way, "Do you feel any internal discomfort when you review your goals?" If you do, then they may be wrong for you, or too far out to be believable.

To what extent are your goals dependent on how well you help other people reach theirs? We develop a wholesome, cleansing, zestful power when we can see how helping others reach their goals will take us to our own.

Setting goals that are harmonious with your values gives your work and life meaning. This brings an exhilaration to the effort you expend and to the work you must do to reach your goals. When your goals and reasons for reaching them are in alignment with your moral compass, you experience high energy. There are no debilitating energy drains or conflicts, and no negative emotions like guilt, anger, anxiety, or low self-esteem. Goals that conflict with our values create stress, emotional clutter, and even neurosis when carried to an extreme.

Salespeople catch fire when they fully desire to create value for others. They get outside themselves. They're stimulated, invigorated, and focused. They feel clean, whole, and significant.

Sense of Worthiness

This deep emotion lies at the heart of our inner beliefs and either blocks or allows our goal achievement.

Inside each of our "I Am" dimensions, etched in stone, are answers to these questions: "How worthy am I?" "What level of goals am I capable of reaching?" "What is my value to my customers?" "What level of rewards, income, and recognition are possible for me to receive?" "What do I deserve to enjoy in life and work rewards?"

With our actions, the answer to these profound questions becomes ingrained without the need for explicit thought. We then, without questioning our actions, engineer our goals, contacts, expectations, and sales results to be consistent with what we deeply believe we deserve to enjoy. We do this unconsciously, without the need for formal, logical mental steps.

Viewing selling as a process of helping and creating value for people enhances our sense of worthiness. Believing that selling is getting people to do something for us, damages it. Again, a paradox. Here's the profound truth: we build self-value to the extent we see ourselves creating value for others. Along this line author Peter Drucker advises, "Stop thinking about what you can achieve; think about what you can contribute."

Sound, solid business advice, or just some babbling?

Peter Drucker doesn't babble!

Supportive Environment

To a large degree we're the product of our environment. We tend to conform to the people, places, and customs around us. All these factors influence us. They have an impact on what we think, the successes we witness, and the customs we feel we have to conform to.

You can structure a success environment in a few practical ways.

First, find one or two people who are achieving goals on the level that you'd like to be enjoying. Ask to learn from them, to become their student. Observe what they do, what they read, how they think. Seek their advice, listen to their success strategies. Find out how they've coped with problems and challenges.

"Why would someone who is already highly successful want to spend time with me?" you ask. Good question. The answer is they would only if they thought you were sincere, and an eager learner. When these people think you really want to learn from them, and *will apply what they teach you,* most will be happy to spend time with you.

Here's a principle I've learned about highly successful people: most high-achieving individuals have a need to perpetuate their success, and will gladly teach those who sincerely want to learn from them.

Another strategy is to align yourself with a small group of people who are interested in high achievement. Find three to five other people with similar values, beliefs, and achievement drives, and meet weekly with them. Spend an hour and follow these suggestions:

1. Each person reports a success principle he or she learned in the past.
2. Relate an example of how they practiced it.
3. Tell what they learned when they put it into practice.

Have one of you assume the leadership role and include each person in sharing their previous three ideas. After all of you have finished sharing your answers to these three points, spend the balance of the time

1. Pointing out strengths you see in each other
2. Sharing examples of other successful people's achievements.

When you conduct these sessions in a totally noncritical environment, where no arguments or disagreements are allowed, you'll soon enjoy the tremendous benefits of personal growth. Talking with others about achievement is a powerful and effective way to increase your own achievement drive.

By far the most powerful influence you can enjoy is to have one person in your life with whom you can share your goals, and know you'll receive total, unconditional acceptance and support. When you have this kind of relationship with your partner, spouse, or friend, you have a power that is unequaled.

When you have a relationship like this you'll enjoy one of life's greatest riches. Few things contribute more to your genuine success, fulfillment, or quality of life than this one-on-one relationship where you can be totally transparent, and be guaranteed complete support, acceptance, and encouragement.

Fortunate indeed is the person who experiences this.

Inner Conflicts Destroy Energy

In our three-dimensional language, it's our "I Think" that leads the way with conscious decisions, choices, and directions. But it's the "I Am" that's the silent command center, and gives or withholds energy to carry out "the best laid plans" that we make. In this way, your "I Am" takes the major authority in your ability to sell.

It's the congruence or conflict between the choices your "I Think" makes and the beliefs and values in your "I Am" that releases or withholds energy.

Remember this model.

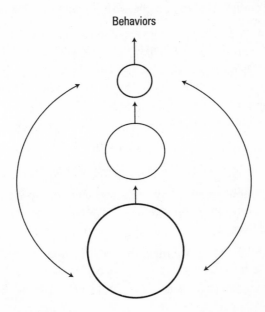

Behaviors

Let me emphasize that our "I Think" is constantly interacting with our "I Am" to produce emotions in our "I Feel." These emotions can either be positive or negative—constructive or destructive. Remember, too, that these produced emotions will most often overrule our conscious volition and produce our behaviors—causing either negative or positive energies to be released.

Carl Jung wrote much about "the wisdom of the unconscious." His belief was that "the spirit of truth" resides in the unconscious dimension within us. He believed that good mental health, or the ability to produce creative energy, happens as there is harmony between our conscious choices, decisions, and actions, and this internal wisdom.

Since achievement drive is positive energy expressed toward productive goals, we must go to the cause in order to produce the effect.

I've seen our course participants by the thousands catch fire and dramatically increase their actual sales and income. They did so because:

- Their view of selling changed.
- They consciously felt good about this new view of selling and intuitively knew they could do it.
- This new view was congruent with their values and self-beliefs in terms of ethics and fair dealing.
- Their conflicts that existed because of old self-focused views of selling fell away.
- They felt clean and fearless about selling in this customer-focused way.
- Their egos were taken out of their line of sight so they could focus on their customers' needs.
- They began to receive more reinforcement, recognition, and appreciation from their customers for their new focus. This caused them to feel good about themselves.

Energy or achievement drive is always increased as we free ourselves emotionally. Expansive emotions of joy, peace, and confidence replace old ones of fear, anxiety, and self-doubting.

To work on our selling we must first learn to work on ourselves.

Symptoms of Inner Conflicts

Let me list some symptoms of internal conflicts that I've noticed in myself and other salespeople.

- *Low Motivation.* Salespeople may set goals, but don't internally view them as possible, so they expend no energy toward their attainment.
- *Resistance to Learn.* People often close their minds to new ideas, information, or skill development if they don't unconsciously feel worthy of higher success.
- *Forced Goals.* When managers impose goals, activities, or ethical standards on salespeople that conflict with their values or perceived skills, salespeople shut down.
- *Goal Diffusion.* Salespeople set too many goals, so they exhibit no focus strong enough to raise their game.
- *Goals in Conflict.* People set goals that demand support of managers, associates, or family members; yet encounter negative situations that hamper their positive efforts.
- *Negative Support Systems.* Having people, places, or things in one's environment that tend to block higher goal achievement by their strong negative influence.
- *Beliefs About Money.* Some people, because of a deeply buried poverty consciousness, feel that it's not right to earn money by selling to friends or family.
- *Low Activity Level.* Salespeople will not make sufficient calls or contacts or call at higher decision levels, regardless of the goals they set, when they have low views of their possibilities or have a sense of unworthiness.

Actually, anytime we set higher goals than we're currently achieving, we immediately trigger internal doubts or conflicts. "Are they possible?" "Can I actually reach them?" "What if I try and fail to reach them?" "What am I going to have to do that's different than what I'm comfortable doing now?" "How am I going to look to my manager if I don't reach these goals?"

These and probably many more questions or concerns can suddenly flood our minds whenever new goals are set, and stop us if we yield to them.

It's the energy, determination, and persistence that's driven by high achievement drive that help us move past these largely self-imposed mental and emotional obstacles.

HOW TO GAIN THE MOST FROM THIS CHAPTER

This chapter holds the key to releasing a whole new energy from within your "I Am." It's potential energy, much like that of a huge pool of oil that's been lying dormant for centuries, undiscovered and untapped.

The suggestions I have shared with you, when approached with a belief that they will get results for you, can help you drill into this pool of potential energy. You'll bring it to the surface and convert it into high-octane fuel that can propel you to new levels of sales and personal success.

To help fuel the release of this energy, you may want to repeat this self-suggestion this week: "I have a compelling need to help as many people as I can."

8 RELEASING UNLIMITED ACHIEVEMENT DRIVE

Assessment

Please take a few moments and check off the number that best describes your present beliefs, boundaries, or behaviors. Use these descriptors as guidelines.

　　　5–Always true, without exception
　　　4–Mostly true
　　　3–True more often than not
　　　2–True only part of the time
　　　1–True only occasionally

1. I resist goal setting because I've done it in the past and it doesn't work.	5 4 3 2 1 | 1 2 3 4 5	1. I continue to set higher sales goals.
2. I tend to focus on what can keep me from reaching my goals.	5 4 3 2 1 | 1 2 3 4 5	2. I tend to focus on the rewards my goals will give me.
3. Achievement is never discussed in my environment.	5 4 3 2 1 | 1 2 3 4 5	3. Achievement is valued in my current environment.
4. I tend to put on a different face when I'm selling.	5 4 3 2 1 | 1 2 3 4 5	4. I am the same person when selling as I am in a regular life situation.
5. I have a problem thinking that I could reach even higher goals.	5 4 3 2 1 | 1 2 3 4 5	5. Achieving higher sales is consistent with my values.
6. I can't share my goals with people because they'll try to shoot them down and discourage me.	5 4 3 2 1 | 1 2 3 4 5	6. I share my goals only with one or two people who I know will unconditionally support me.
7. I don't set goals that I don't think I can reach.	5 4 3 2 1 | 1 2 3 4 5	7. I set challenging but realistic goals and then figure out a way to reach them.
8. Making sales is just part of my work; I'm the same whether I do or don't.	5 4 3 2 1 | 1 2 3 4 5	8. I get a real "high" when I make a sale.

9. More often than not obstacles have stopped me from reaching my goals.	5 4 3 2 1	1 2 3 4 5	9. I get through most obstacles that get in my way of reaching goals.
10. The thing I like the least about selling is the uncertainty of it.	5 4 3 2 1	1 2 3 4 5	10. I love the challenges and opportunities that selling gives me.

- Add up the numbers in the right-hand column. _____
- Add up the numbers in the left-hand column. _____
- Subtract the left-hand column total from the right-hand column total and score yourself. _____

Assessments scoring guide is on page 35.

Keeping Score—Chapter 8

Behavior that gets evaluated, gets improved.

On a scale of 1–10, please evaluate your performance of each of these parts of the Breakthrough Process.

	S	M	T	W	T	F	S
1. I reviewed or revised my goals today.							
2. I reviewed the six steps for building my view of my goal possibilities today.							
3. I took time to think how my selling is consistent with my values.							
4. I focused on creating value for customers today, and I allowed myself to feel worthy of higher rewards.							
5. I took one action toward building a supportive environment today.							
Total Each Day							

9 **Control**

Handling the Emotional Side of Selling

"I WENT INTO A PERSONAL MELTDOWN LAST SEPTEMBER," one of our course graduates wrote me. "I hit bottom so hard before this class started that on a self-administered psychological test rating of 'suicidal' at a zero, 'suicidal thoughts' at one, and 'emotionally well adjusted' at ten, I was a *two*. Previously I'd never experienced depression. I could not even move for five weeks.

"I then enrolled in your course, Managing Goal Achievement, so emotionally shaken that I wondered what I was doing in it.

"I realized that, while I'd been successful, I was trying to reach goals that weren't mine, but rather other people's goals. They wanted me to accomplish *their* goals for *their* happiness. I must have spent about twenty hours the next day thinking what I should be doing.

"I put together a plan for a new career. With the start of Goal Clarity and living up to my values, I have a renewed understanding of my view of my possibilities. This course gave me the supportive environment, bringing my life into congruence.

"I pulled out of my depressed state so fast that the people around me questioned the depths of my recovery.

"I want to thank you for the development of the course," the young salesperson concluded.

I flew to the city where this course was conducted, and met this man. He is real, and his story is true. His facilitator validated it, and I've kept up with the fellow ever since.

How fragile our emotions are! How illogical they are. How exhilarating. How numbing. How uplifting. How deflating. How unpredictable.

Many factors influence your emotions. As a salesperson, you're subjected to many more ups and downs than most people—acceptances and rejections. While you can't always control these life events, you can control your responses to them, thereby controlling your emotions.

To the degree you control your emotions you'll succeed or fail in selling. It's that simple!

But controlling your emotions isn't simple. It's difficult at times. Talent, knowledge, and even willpower acquiesce to these unpredictable surges of internal eruptions. Shakespeare put it so well in *Hamlet* when he said, "Thus conscience does make cowards of us all."

I understand that.

I was twenty-one and had just graduated from college. My first job was as an outside salesman for an office equipment company. I was calling on purchasing agents and office managers who were two to three times my age.

I still remember Mr. Stanley, who was the purchasing agent for a large grain company. I also remember driving around and around the block, where his building was, hoping I *wouldn't* find a parking spot.

My mind was flooded with my last few experiences of calling on him. He usually kept me waiting in the reception room, which gave me more time to build up my nervousness. I'd be ushered into his office. He wouldn't stand up or allow me to shake his hand. He wouldn't say a word, but just stare and glare at me. In my emotional frustration I'd start talking—telling him about a particular product I thought he might be interested in buying.

With the coldest eyes, and blandest face I'd ever seen, he'd sit there not saying a word. He'd reach into his shirt pocket, pull out a Pall Mall cigarette, and hold it between his thumb and index finger, rolling it around. Tobacco would dribble out of the end of the cigarette, as he held it up in front of his eyes, while staring at me.

Man, talk about weird!

He'd then poke the other end of the cigarette in his mouth, flick his Zippo lighter, and torch the end of it where the tobacco had fallen out from the paper. The paper would flare up, he'd put his lighter on his desk, stand up, brush the tobacco off his lap, and dismiss me.

I'd stumble out of the building, emotionally emasculated.

What was going on here?

Let's consider—the facts logically.

I was twenty-one, six foot two inches tall, strong, having done construction work during my college summers. Mr. Stanley was probably close to sixty years old. He was pale, emaciated-looking, had a bad smoker's cough, and could hardly lift his Zippo lighter.

So why was I so intimidated by him? I could have wiped him out with one hand.

The reality was that my emotions were not under the direct control of my logic, size, or strength. I might as well have been a ninety-seven-pound weakling, and him King Kong.

Emotional Responses Are Natural

I've known a few salespeople who appeared to have no negative emotions: no fear of rejection, no call reluctance, no approach anxiety. Usually they also have little empathy, or the ability to read other people's emotional responses. Their inner "feelers" are sealed off. So what seems to be an asset on one hand is a liability on the other. The lack of sensitivity that protects them from fear of rejection also blocks them from connecting with people in deeper emotional ways.

So, something is missing.

Most highly successful salespeople have a balance of two major skills:

1. Empathy, or the ability to understand and interpret the feelings of their customers,
2. Achievement drive, or the desire to get results and enjoy the fruits of their efforts.

Highly effective salespeople have these two traits in balance. When out of balance, salespeople can have these problems:

1. High empathy, low drive—lacks initiative to get results, possibly socializing too much.
2. High empathy, high drive—the ideal balance for sustained sales success and customer relationships.
3. Low empathy, low drive—will fail at selling.

HIGH

High empathy Low achievement drive	High empathy High achievement drive
Low empathy Low achievement drive	Low empathy High achievement drive

Empathy

LOW   Achievement Drive   HIGH

4. Low empathy, high drive—will run over people, burn relationships, and suffer stress.

My observation is that people with high empathy and low achievement drive may have more *concerns* about acceptance from customers. Their thoughts could be:

Will I be able to connect with this person?

Will they understand me and my intentions?

Will they accept or reject me?

Will I be able to handle their questions or responses?

Will I be able to see them on a favorable basis?

These concerns can take us into two emotional directions—positive or negative. They can cause fear of rejection, call reluctance, or nervousness. But they can also produce confidence, enthusiasm, and anticipation. Our own purpose, and view of selling, colors our perceptions. The following *purposes* then create positive or negative emotions within us.

I need to make this sale.

I hope I can convince them to buy from me.

I'm not sure I can handle this size account.

I'm mainly concerned about making my quota this month, and hope this will help.

I hear that this person is really tough on salespeople.

I'm not sure whether or not I can help them, but I owe it to them to see if I can.

The purpose of my call is just to get to know them and understand their business a bit better.

I have no need to impress them; I just want to ask questions and listen.

I'm confident that I can help them solve major problems they have.

I'm convinced that my product or service will create more value for them than they're currently enjoying.

Carefully analyze these purposes of your contacts. See how different they are. Then understand that it's our *purpose,* and view of selling, when experiencing situations that creates our emotions.

Looking at it logically, it's our selling concerns flowing through our selling purpose that trigger our emotions; that then influences our behaviors.

Look at it like this.

Concerns $\longrightarrow$ Purpose $\longrightarrow$ Emotions $\longrightarrow$ Behavior

I had high calling anxiety, or reluctance, until I changed my view of selling. As long as I viewed it as getting people to do something for me, I couldn't shake the involuntary emotion. But when I began to view it as helping create value for people—if they wanted or needed my help—my whole emotional response changed. My purpose predicted my performance.

How could I have had fear of rejection when all I was trying to do was help people, if they wanted help? When my attitude was, "I'm here to help them, if they need and want help," it freed me up emotionally.

Wrong Purpose Creates Negative Emotions

So it's our purpose for contacting people that colors the resulting emotion, not the actual situation or circumstance itself.

Go back and read the first five of the ten preceding statements. Look at the first one: "I need to make this sale." That concern can cause most salespeople to experience emotional conflicts when they view selling as getting people to do something for them. It also elicits emotions of doubt, fear, and sweaty palms—the "What if they don't like me or buy from me" level of anxiety. Or, the emotions triggered when we think, "What bad things are going to happen if I don't make this sale?" To the extent we ask these kinds of questions, we'll shut down and retreat to avoidance behaviors.

On the other hand, if our purpose is to help create value for people, where our old concern was, "I need to make this sale," We'll now say, "I need to help these people—if they want help." This changed purpose causes us to ask such questions as, "Who has a need I can fill?" "Who can I create value for?" "Who has a problem I can help solve?" "How can I best solve their problem, and create the most value for them?"

Have this purpose of selling and you'll be highly motivated, energized, and confident when contacting people.

See the difference our purpose makes in influencing our emotions and resulting behaviors?

Moments of Truth Arouse Emotional Conflicts

As long as goals, calls for appointments, actual contacts, presentations, negotiations, and closes are in the future, few internal conflicts are aroused. But the closer the time is for these steps to be done, the more emotions increase to the degree that we need to make a sale.

For example, when I need to make a sale—because I need the money or to fill a quota—and I get close to the action point, heavy emotions are triggered. They often involve fear—I'm afraid they won't buy, and am concerned about how I can handle the consequences. "If they don't buy, I can't pay my house payment!" "If I can't make the sale, I may lose my job!"

The emotions that these moments of truth trigger are then filtered through our values, views of selling, views of abilities, and beliefs in the efficacy of our products. The resulting emotions then trigger certain behaviors. It all happens involuntarily.

So forget "trying harder," discipline, or being "tough-minded" in dealing with fear of rejection or call reluctance. Go to the cause and change it. The *cause* is your purpose—to see if people have needs they want filled, that you can help them fill.

Emotional Tensile Strength

Just as the tensile strength of metal allows it to be bent over and over, and still retain its form, our emotions are the same way. Can we handle the concerns, uncertainties, and repeated rejections that selling presents to us?

Let me quickly make it clear that this doesn't involve "fighting through" the negative emotional feelings we experience. Rather, it involves changing the way we think—how we explain events to ourselves when we experience rejection, frustration, or down times. We must understand that it's not the actual circumstances that energize or stop us, it's our perception of them and reaction to them.

Martin E. P. Seligman wrote in *Learned Optimism*, "One of the most significant findings in psychology in the last twenty years is that individuals can change the way they think." He advises, "We must change what we tell ourselves when we fail. We must change the way we explain negative events to ourselves."

I'll take that a second step—we must also change the way we explain success to ourselves.

How Do You Explain Situations to Yourself?

The way you explain selling situations and results to yourself is the key to developing strong emotional tensile strength. What do you tell yourself when you succeed? What do you tell yourself when you're rejected? Your responses in these situations will determine much of your success.

Let's take a look at some different selling situations where your emotions are involved. We'll look at two ways of explaining these to ourselves. I realize that you may or may not do all these steps, but for an overall look, let's consider them.

PHONING FOR APPOINTMENTS. For many salespeople this is the first "sweaty palms" experience. The first opportunity to be rejected or accepted. Of either getting through or not being able to talk to the right person.

This is the moment that many salespeople sit and stare at the telephone, and the longer they stare, the more emotional perspiration pours off them.

Here are a couple of thoughts that you choose to think:

- "I'm afraid I can't get through or this person may not want to talk to me!"
- "I'm sure if this person knew how much I could help him, he'd look forward to seeing me!"

YOUR INITIAL APPROACH. Whether in person or on the telephone you can often be concerned about whether or not you can connect with people. You know the importance of your approach with people, and it's normal to be concerned about your receptivity. Your thoughts might be closely akin to either of these:

- "Who is this person and will I be able to communicate with her?"
- "I'm anxious to meet this person, and I have confidence in my ability to sincerely ask questions about her interests and then just listen."

YOUR INTERVIEW. When your objective is to ask open-ended questions to determine if this person has a want, need, problem, or goal you can help him reach or satisfy, you'll have little emotional conflict.

But if your objective is to ask him leading questions to set him up so you can get him to buy, your emotional conflict rises. So these attitudes or objectives create different emotions.

- "Will I be able to sell him my product or service?"

- "I will ask appropriate questions so I can understand his needs, wants, problems, or goals that he wants filled, solved, or reached."

At this point your honest attitude should be, "It's not my purpose at this time to try to sell him my product or service, rather to see if he has a need my product or service will fill or solve."

DEMONSTRATING. This is the time you present your solution to the needs that have been admitted in your interview. Should no needs be admitted, you don't do a "show and tell." You just say, "It's apparent that you have no need for my product or service, so it would be inappropriate for me to take your time in explaining it."

But this isn't the way most salespeople do it, is it?

In product-focused selling, the salespeople spend little or no time in discovering if needs exist; instead they move quickly into a product demonstration or explanation. This then elicits the fear question of "What if I can't convince him to buy from me?"

Contrast this with the intent, "I will only recommend my product or service if it best fits this person's needs."

When you wouldn't recommend your product or service, unless it would truly fill their needs and create value for them, you look professional, reduce any fear of not making a sale, and retain strong confidence. And as I've stressed many times in this book, you sell more this way.

VALIDATING. It's here that you show proof of your product's effectiveness, as well as develop trust between you and your customer. This all begins by asking yourself and affirmatively answering, "Is my solution the best one for this person?"

People tend to trust us when we're the kind of people they can trust. To become the kind of person people can trust, we get back to practicing ethical values like:

- *I do the right thing because it's the right thing to do.*
- *I tell the truth in all situations unless it would be hurtful to others.*

When these and other values pop into our minds in different selling situations, and we allow them to guide our behaviors, we'll be the kind of people that customers can trust.

NEGOTIATION. Many people see negotiation as a process of convincing customers to see things our way—to change their minds. But who of us want other people attempting to change our minds? The moment we detect their intent, we throw up all kinds of resistance.

Here are two opposing questions or thoughts that we might think when in a negotiating posture.

- "How do I get this person to see things the way I want him to see them?"
- "How can I better understand things from her perspective, so I can work out a win-win solution?"

Big difference, isn't it?

CLOSING. Here's where we simply ask for a decision at the right time. The right time is when all the previous AID, Inc. steps have been completed.

In the perfect world of AID, Inc. you should know what the answer will be before you ask for a decision. Often though, when all the other five steps have been successfully done, your customer will ask you to take the appropriate closing action. So your customer does the close step, rather than it being something you do.

At this point you're asking yourself questions like:

- "Is this the best solution for this person's needs, wants, goals, or problems?"
- "Does my customer believe my recommendation is the right one for him?"

But in the real world, many salespeople have thoughts like, "I'm afraid to ask for a decision, because I'm afraid they'll say 'No,' and I don't want to get that answer." It's here that salespeople aren't confident in the value they'll give customers and probably have been very product-focused. They haven't done a thorough interview or asked good questions to understand customers' concerns or feelings.

If you've completed all the AID, Inc. steps, *you know* if your offering is the best solution for your customer. You also know that *your customer knows* it will satisfy her needs. So you can sincerely say to yourself, "This will satisfy this customer's wants or needs and give her value beyond what she expects to get."

This sincere belief drives your confidence and makes asking for a decision an act of serving your customer's best interests, rather than expecting her to serve yours.

As you think about these different selling situations, what do you naturally say to yourself before or when you experience them?

What you say to yourself will trigger a corresponding emotion.

Look back over the statements or questions I listed in the different sales situations. Which ones do you instinctively say to yourself at that time? What would you like to naturally say to yourself when these times occur?

Go back and identify one specific situation (calling for appointments, negotiating, closing, etc.) and write a statement that says what you'd intuitively like to say to yourself at that time. Then begin repeating this self-suggestion over and over to yourself. Visualize yourself in actual situations saying that. Picture and feel the new emotion of confidence that you'll enjoy.

With work on this, you'll gradually change what you say to yourself from negative to positive statements. And as this occurs, your emotions will begin to change, which will soon cause you to increase your confidence, professionalism, and energy.

Projecting Possible Rejection or Acceptance

As you go back and read these previous different sales scenarios, and analyze positive thoughts you can say to yourself when facing these separate steps of the sales process, you'll begin to increase your emotional tensile strength. In time you'll develop unconscious thought habits.

In simple terms, we're all preconditioned to think positively or negatively in these situations. To either expect acceptance or rejection. Since these responses have been developed by past programming, they can be changed with new programming.

Please stop and mull over what I've just said.

The question—*the question*—is, "How do you automatically think in these different sales steps?" Positively or negatively? Optimistically or pessimistically? How you think—the kind of customer reaction you unconsciously expect at these points—is probably influencing your sales more than anything else.

Seligman writes, "Habits of thinking need not be forever." He asks, "What if the traditional view of the components of success is wrong?" "What if the third factor—optimism or pessimism—matters as much as talent or desire?"

Whether we think optimistically or pessimistically, each is a cause that's automatically driving a certain effect. We'll think pessimistically when our view of selling conflicts with our view of our abilities or our values. We can best think optimistically, in our sales roles, when these dimensions are in congruence.

By internalizing the chapters of this book and understanding and practicing the AID, Inc. selling system, you'll bring the five dimensions of the Sales Congruence Model into harmony. By application of the Action Guides I give you, you'll naturally develop more positive automatic thoughts, expectations, and responses.

Remember that your thinking patterns change as you choose to practice customer-focused sales behaviors. These conscious choices then interact with the values, "spirit of truth," and views of abilities in your "I Am" dimension to produce confidence, optimism, and higher energy.

Emotional Control

Dan Goleman, in his excellent book *Working with Emotional Intelligence*, makes this case: "For star performers in all jobs, in every field, emotional competence is twice as important as purely cognitive abilities."

Keeping steady emotions is a highly successful trait for all salespeople. Being able to stay on a level emotional plane, despite failures or successes, separates the losers from the winners.

As I've observed many salespeople perform, I've noticed that a vast majority of them don't know how to handle defeats *or* successes.

A Balanced View of Selling

For our emotions to be most positive, we must have a balanced view of selling. An emotionally healthy salesperson has a balanced view of selling that looks like this:

1. *My main purpose is to create value for my customers.*
2. *My secondary purpose is to be rewarded consistently with the value I create for them.*

Think about this balance a moment. It gives you confidence and energy and builds a prosperity consciousness.

Your self-esteem is influenced.

Self-Esteem Quadrants

There are two thinking patterns that, when in balance, have lots to do with our values, self-esteem, and success in selling.

1. *I view selling as creating value for you.*
2. *I view selling as creating value for me.*

Notice the quadrants in the model on page 184 and how they might affect our self-esteem.

As you look at this model, ask yourself, "How would each quadrant influence . . ."

Our purpose for selling

Customers' trust of us

Customer satisfaction

Our personal confidence

Our professionalism

Our long-term success

Our energy and emotional tensile strength

Self- Esteem Quadrants Model

HIGH

"I view selling as just creating value for you, but not me."	"I view selling as creating value for both you and me."
"I view selling as creating value neither for you nor for me."	"I view selling as just creating value for me, but not you."

Selling Is Helping You

LOW   **Selling Is Helping Me**   HIGH

Our view of self

Our view of customers

Our desire to learn and grow

Our achievement drive

Our prosperity or poverty consciousness

Interesting speculation, isn't it?

Developing Confidence in Selling

The Quadrant 2 emotional balance is the healthiest of all. The following beliefs, combined together, form a balance.

1. *Selling is creating value for you.*
   - "I want to understand your needs, wants, problems, or goals."
   - "My focus is on creating value for you."
   - "I want to help you succeed."
   - "I will focus on giving you more value than you pay me for."

- "I value our relationship."
- "I value you as an important person."

2. *Selling is creating value for me, too.*
   - "I'm content to be rewarded consistently with the value I give you."
   - "When I give you extra value I know I'll be compensated one way or another."
   - "I have a healthy view of the rewards I should enjoy as a result of the service I give."
   - "I have a strong win-win philosophy in my sales career."
   - "I set high goals for my sales with the quiet confidence that I'll reach them because of the high level of service I give my customers."
   - "I value me as a person who creates high value for customers."

With desire, practice, and time you can program this balanced confidence-building process into your "I Am."

HOW TO GAIN THE MOST FROM THIS CHAPTER

To develop this balanced view of selling, which will build your own self-esteem and emotional tensile strength, here are some suggestions:

1. Get a full intellectual understanding of what this balance consists of.
2. Decide if you believe it's the right way to think.
3. Select one statement under each of the previous two ways of viewing selling, and write them on cards.
4. Under each self-suggestion write a specific action or behavior you'll do to carry it out.
5. Review your cards each day and practice your action step when you have the opportunity.

With sincere intent, practice, and evaluation you'll soon begin to develop a balanced view of the way you sell. As this balance builds and grows you'll notice a big difference in your self-esteem and confidence levels. Your natural fears of rejection, contact avoidance, or reluctance to promote yourself will begin to die.

So rather than using willpower, discipline, or trying harder, work on the cause—your inner values, beliefs, and views of a balanced, win-win career objective.

You learned that your emotions drive your external behaviors, and the degree of your emotions is defined by your purpose when you meet a specific challenge. So it's having the appropriate purpose that produces positive emotions, rather than using discipline or willpower to deal with the negative emotions.

This self-suggestion will help you drill this belief deep within your "I Am": "When I control my purpose and responses I control my success."

Change your beliefs about selling and you'll automatically convert your responses and resulting behaviors into more positive, confident ones.

To the degree you control your emotions you'll succeed or fail in selling. The moment you begin to do this you'll enjoy increased confidence, hope for the future, and genuine optimism.

You'll never again be the same.

9 HANDLING THE EMOTIONAL SIDE OF SELLING

Assessment

Please take a few moments and check off the number that best describes your present beliefs, boundaries, or behaviors. Use these descriptors as guidelines.

> 5–Always true, without exception
> 4–Mostly true
> 3–True more often than not
> 2–True only part of the time
> 1–True only occasionally

1. I'm mainly concerned with how my customers will like or accept me.	5 4 3 2 1 1 2 3 4 5	1. I'm mainly concerned with understanding my customers.
2. I'm often afraid I can't communicate well with customers.	5 4 3 2 1 1 2 3 4 5	2. I feel confident in my social skills with customers.

3. I focus too much on how I'll be able to respond to the questions and concerns customers might have.	5 4 3 2 1	1 2 3 4 5	3. My main focus is on listening to and understanding my customers.
4. When contacting people my main objective is to sell them something.	5 4 3 2 1	1 2 3 4 5	4. When contacting people my main objective is to understand their needs or goals.
5. I'm always afraid my customers won't buy from me or like me.	5 4 3 2 1	1 2 3 4 5	5. I'm always excited to see if I can bring value to a customer.
6. I tend to fear customers' concerns or objections and see them in negative lights.	5 4 3 2 1	1 2 3 4 5	6. I ask for and welcome customers' concerns or objections when I'm explaining my products or service.
7. I view customers' concerns as reasons why they might not want to buy.	5 4 3 2 1	1 2 3 4 5	7. I view customers' concerns as positive signs of their interest.
8. I view closing a sale as mainly benefiting me.	5 4 3 2 1	1 2 3 4 5	8. I view closing a sale as benefiting both my customers and me.
9. When I don't close a sale I blame myself for being a weak closer.	5 4 3 2 1	1 2 3 4 5	9. When I don't close a sale I believe that it wasn't the right solution at the right time.
10. I often allow customers' negative responses to trigger negative emotions within me.	5 4 3 2 1	1 2 3 4 5	10. I allow customers' negative emotions to remain theirs and not influence my responses.

- Add up the numbers in the right-hand column.   _____
- Add up the numbers in the left-hand column.   _____
- Subtract the left-hand column total from the right-hand column total and score yourself.   _____

Assessments scoring guide is on page 35.

Keeping Score—Chapter 9

Behavior that gets evaluated, gets improved.

On a scale of 1–10, please evaluate your performance of each of these Action Guides.

	S	M	T	W	T	F	S
1. I demonstrated my belief that selling is identifying needs people have and creating value for them.							
2. I practiced an AID, Inc. customer-focused action today.							
3. I examined my values as I interacted with people today.							
4. I focused on creating value for everyone I contacted today.							
5. I greeted customers' concerns as ways to understand and serve them better today.							
Total Each Day							

10 Social Skills
Helping People Feel Understood

ONCE I WAS CONDUCTING A TWO-DAY SALES SEMINAR FOR an international organization. At the end of the first day, the VP of sales, who had hired me, came up and said, "I know you're tired. Let's get away from the crowd and have an early, quiet dinner."

That sounded good to me, and we went to a quiet, elegant French restaurant, where soothing piano music played.

During the meal he mentioned that his son was going through a divorce, and was having some struggles adjusting to it. He explained in great detail the emotional challenges his son was experiencing. He asked several questions, and after a couple of hours wanted to know if I would talk to his son the next time I was in the city.

I agreed to do it and told him when I'd be through next. He said he'd get us together. I made it clear that I wasn't a professional counselor, and he nodded and replied that he just thought I'd connect with his son.

Within a short time I scheduled an evening layover in his city and he picked me up. As I got in his car, he exited the airport and said, "I told you that I wanted you to talk to my son?"

"Yeah," I replied.

"Well, it's not him I want you to talk to, it's me!"

"I kinda thought so," I replied.

I then spent the rest of the evening just listening to him. It was clear to me that he wasn't really looking to me for advice; he just wanted someone to listen to him. He simply needed to vent his anger, anxiety, and other the feelings he didn't understand that churned inside him.

All I did was listen, and occasionally ask him questions that got him

187

explaining his feelings more deeply. After that I did a lot of work for his company, and we became good friends. He was a very bright, strong, capable, seemingly tough-minded executive—who needed to talk to someone he felt he could trust. He had no one in his life to fill this role.

He had a very common need.

"Help Me Feel Understood"

This is the silent plea of most people. Not only does effective listening help others feel that we understand them, but it also helps them understand themselves. It cuts both ways.

I've found few other skills as helpful in selling as delivering this need to people. It can set us apart from our competition and make us valuable to our clients in a way that's hard to duplicate.

Allow me to draw a distinction between understanding people and helping them feel understood. This suggests a much deeper level of communication than most people think about.

It also spotlights the reason why many people buy. As we think about this let's contrast *why people buy* with *how we sell*. This suggests a subtle, yet incredibly powerful difference. Do we approach the selling process as one that helps people buy, or one that helps us sell?

I began learning this incredibly valuable lesson many years ago from a very wise man. J. Henry Thompson was a regional manager for Diebold, Inc. After witnessing me botch a couple of calls by talking too much, he gave me advice I've never forgotten. He said, as we got into my car, "You know, Ron, you might want to ask people questions and do a lot of listening, rather than doing all the talking."

His understated advice hit me like a rock. Immediately, my past sales call mistakes flashed before me. It also caused me to realize that if he had wanted to elaborate more on my lack of wisdom, he could have found much more to point out.

I respected him so much that I immediately began to approach people by asking questions about things that might interest them. I began to see how quickly I could get people talking and me listening. And very soon, my customers began to buy more from me. It took a while for me to realize that I was getting people to want to buy from me, rather than trying to sell them things.

I discovered that each customer had things they wanted to talk to me about, more than they wanted to talk about office equipment and supplies. My listening helped develop strong relationships. It dawned upon me that much of what I was selling could be purchased from several other salespeople or companies; but developing relationships with customers caused them to want to buy from me.

In time I had customers sharing some of their deepest personal problems with me. Problems with their children, other employees, or their bosses. Often they would close their doors, or take me to coffee just to talk.

I discovered that everyone has a need to talk about their problems, concerns, joys, hobbies, or special interests. The secret was knowing the right questions to ask, and then being a good listener. And . . . keeping what we hear inside our heads, and not allowing it to escape out through our mouths.

As I began listening to people, I discovered many interesting things about them. It was fascinating to widen my understanding of different people. At the time I didn't fully grasp what was happening; I just felt closer to people, and they seemed to trust me and buy more from me.

It took time to learn that there was still another communication level to attain. Not only did I need to understand people, but I finally got it that I must help them *feel understood.*

Not just listen, but help people feel understood.

The Power of Empathy

We begin to see now the real reasons why people want to do business with us—as salespeople, we become an extension of them. In a sense we become a part of them and their world as we develop empathy and rapport with them.

Empathy is feeling *with* another person. It's seeing the world through their eyes and viewing it as they view it. It's understanding how and why they think what they think. It's a direct connection between my "I Am" and another person's "I Am." It isn't a conscious logical act. In its deepest form it bypasses our logical, intellectual levels and connects our minds, hearts, and souls. It implies understanding and responding to the uniqueness of other people.

Paradoxically, genuine empathy carries its own validation. When we sincerely care about other people and want to understand them, we make ourselves important to them in a deeply profound way.

Empathy is an active force. It breaks down barriers, cements relationships, and attracts people to us. It silently moves us past people's outer defenses, nourishes their deep sense of value, and causes them to say, "You're important to me!" "You add to my life!" "You help me become someone I couldn't be without you!"

Successful Selling Is Being Important to People

Here's the paradox: customers want you to be important to them more than they want to be important to you.

After all, they have this right. They're the customer.

Professional salespeople know that purchase decisions are often driven by their own sincerity and genuine interest in their customers. They silently seek to understand things about their customers, such as:

Who are you?

What are you thinking?

How are you feeling?

What's important to you?

How can I best understand you?

What do you want from our relationship?

Could it be that many people want to buy from *you*, because of *who* you are, before they want to buy from you because of *what* you're selling?

Action Guides for Effective Communication

Let's get away from the conceptual and get down to the here-and-now, practical, everyday interactions with customers.

Here are some basic Action Guides. When they're done with a sincere intent to understand customers so you can serve them in the greatest way, will take you to a high level of success.

1. Ask open-ended, indirect questions that draw out people's wants, needs, opinions, and feelings.
2. Listen without biases, distractions, or interruptions.
3. Understand what people say and why they say it.
4. Paraphrase your understanding back to customers and make sure they feel understood.

Ask Open-Ended, Indirect Questions

Remember, there are several reasons why people will buy your product or service. Here are a few.

They want to own it.

They want the end-result benefits it will give them.

They want to experience certain positive feelings as a result of buying it.

They want to achieve a specific goal by having it.

They want to eliminate certain risks by having it.

They want to impress others by having it.

They want to enjoy some specific gratification by having it.

They want to overcome or prevent certain problems by having it.

They want others to feel good about them, because they have it.

They want to feel understood by you and others.

These give you an idea of the different motivations people have when making purchase decisions from you. Your job, as much as possible, is to determine these motives in your fact-finding interview, and conversations. Your skillful use of appropriate questions helps you do this.

Your Reason for Asking

Your motive in asking questions usually influences the answers you get. If your reason is to get information so you can understand your customers' needs, why they want these needs filled, and the desired gratification, your sincerity will be communicated. But if your objective is to get them to do what you want them to do, and you ask leading questions, they'll smell this out also.

When you sincerely ask questions with the genuine intent to understand a customer's needs, you send the message that you value the person, that it's her needs you're there to understand. Empathy, rapport, trust, and an emotional bonding takes place as this exchange happens. In this type of social interaction, psychological value is being communicated back and forth.

To the extent that you give psychological value to people, they'll usually be impelled to return that to you. We call this the Law of Psychological Reciprocity. It means that most people are instinctively impelled to return the same level of value to us as we've given them. Value here is trust, respect, and interest in them and their needs.

This exchange of value works through subconscious levels. It causes them to be more open to us. To be more receptive to our ideas, solutions, or opinions.

ASK DIFFERENT QUESTIONS IN DIFFERENT SALES STEPS To help you fully understand people, and help them feel understood, here are some different questions you can ask in the AID, Inc. sales steps.

Approach: Ask nonthreatening, get-them-talking-and-you-listening questions. If it's your first meeting, ask what work they do, how long they've been in their jobs, about their family, hobbies, or special interests.

"How did you get in this line of work?" "What do you like most about it?" "How long have you lived in this city?" These and other nonthreatening questions get people quickly talking and you listening.

If you're seeing customers on an ongoing basis, you can ask about things they've previously shared with you—their child's little league game, vacation, husband's health, etc.

Your purpose is to simply get them talking about themselves and you listening. Obviously, you'll do this differently with different people. Some people want to talk about some subjects more than others.

Interview: It's here that you want to identify needs, wants, problems, and goals they have that you can help them reach or satisfy. You want to know what their *desired situation* is, as contrasted with their *current situation*. You ask appropriate questions that get them talking about both of these. As they explain, you listen and respond to their answers. You ask clarifying questions as they give you information. You paraphrase what they tell you and give them feedback that you understand them.

When a customer admits a gap between where they now are and where they'd like to be and that creates a conflict or dissonance, you'll want to go further with more questions. Should they not admit a difference between where they now are and where they'd like to be, you may not have a good prospect.

But when there is an admission, you want to understand the rewards, or gratification they want to enjoy.

Then, you'll want to ask questions about the *consequences* of not taking action. In no case are you putting pressure on them. All you're doing is getting them to think and give you information.

When we make a purchase decision we consciously or unconsciously contrast where we are now with where we'd like to be. If there's a gap, we then visualize the rewards of making the purchase, or the consequences of not making it. This includes everything from buying popcorn at a movie to a new automobile or home.

There's a powerful persuasion principle involved here: people are more apt to accept new ideas they discover for themselves than when you try to tell or convince them. Said another way, people usually become more rigid and closed when they perceive we're trying to get them to change their minds or accept new ideas.

This interviewing process works best when you have a sincere intent to assist your customers in thinking through their situation, rather than getting them to arrive at a conclusion that you want.

Demonstration: In your presentation phase, you want to ask demonstration-response questions. These are ones that ask for feedback about how your product or service fills the admitted needs of your customers. Questions such as, "How do you like this feature?" "Will this give you the benefits you want?" "What questions do you have?"

Validation: To complete this step you'll want to observe customers' body language, responses, openness, or concerns that haven't been addressed in their minds. You want customers to believe you, trust you, and feel comfortable with you. They may want more evidence of results on third-party endorsements.

Negotiation: To successfully work through problems or concerns you want to know, "What concerns do you have that we need to discuss?" In other words, bring to the surface anything that might be clogging their willingness to make a purchase decision. These issues are easier to deal with at this point than left uncovered. Unless they're understood, they'll probably cause your customers to say "No" to your closing question.

Attempt to get all objections, concerns, or possible roadblocks out of the way.

Welcome objections. You want objections, concerns, or problems that would keep them from making a positive purchase decision, to surface. When they do, you want to ask, "Is this challenge something that you want to work out?" If they say, "Yes," you then proceed to help them work it out. Otherwise, you're not going to successfully close.

When you work out their concerns, and they have no more, you then ask for a decision. Often, though, before you ask, they've told you they want to proceed.

When you learn the different types of questions to ask at specific sales intervals, you are truly customer-focused.

Listen Without Biases, Distractions, or Interruptions

The psychological power of listening has an incredible influence upon your selling success. In the psychology of persuasion, listening plays the keynote. You *listen* people into buying much more than you *talk* them into buying.

Listening is a lost art for many salespeople. It's synonymous with customer-focused selling. It often doesn't exist when people do product- or transaction-focused selling. Have you ever noticed how different people listen, or fail to listen? Here are several observations I've made. People listen:

> To understand
>
> To make people feel understood
>
> To clarify their own thinking
>
> To rehearse what they're going to say when the other person finally shuts up
>
> To hear what we want to hear
>
> To constantly interrupt people
>
> To wait for others to pause or take a breath, so they can begin talking
>
> To interrupt others and tell them what we think they're trying to tell us (that one really gets me)
>
> To listen with a resistant, biased viewpoint
>
> To allow themselves time to replay last Saturday's golf game while the customer's talking

Well, you've noticed other ways people listen or don't listen.

Do a little research project for yourself. Observe the next ten people with whom you communicate. See how many really listen to you. Or notice a small group of people talking. See who listens and who doesn't. Notice the body language and facial expressions of all the people in the groups.

When you listen to people, plug in and really listen. Get eye contact if it's in person. Visualize yourself looking into people's eyes even when talking over the telephone. This gives you a focus. Notice their responses—what they do with their hands, eyes, gestures, and facial expressions. All these are communication signals you can pick up when you listen.

Understand the *What* and *Why*

Very often what people say isn't what they really mean. For instance, customers often tell you *what* they want to buy, but rarely tell you *why* they want it. There's a big difference. But buyers are motivated more because of the why than the what.

Try to buy a car, and the salespeople will probably attempt to sell you a car—thinking that it's the specific car you want to buy. But you don't just want the car to have a car, you want it for a specific reason—styling, color, price, gas mileage, resale value, etc.

Not many salespeople know that it's the why you want it that motivates you. Professional, customer-focused salespeople know this, and always attempt to understand why a customer wants to buy, not just what.

To discover the *why* people purchase whatever you're selling, you can use several subtle ways. Ask questions like, "How will you use this?" "To what occasion will you wear it?" "Who will you enjoy sharing your new home with?" "Who will you want to be the first to ride in your new car?" "How often do you entertain?"

Questions like these help you understand why people want what you're selling. Professionals are able to dig deeper and ask sensitive questions that help them understand this.

Paraphrase Your Understanding and Make Sure Customers Feel Understood

As you ask questions, make sure you actively listen and understand *what* people say. When they answer your questions, give them feedback that lets them know you understood them. You can do this by paraphrasing your understanding of what they told you.

Paraphrasing is saying, "If I understand your needs, you want a home with . . ." Here you explain what you heard them say. Then, if you can, also give feedback about your understanding of why they want it. "You like this floor plan, because you entertain a lot, and the kitchen and patio are perfect for that."

Paraphrasing is a powerful way to give positive reinforcement to people. It builds emotional bridges. It shows you value your customer's opinions, beliefs, expressed wants or needs. You can also paraphrase people's objections or concerns—restate them and ask if you understood them correctly. Do this, before you answer the objection. Let them know you understand it, and that they have been understood. This shows that you appreciate their point of view and aren't trying to dismiss or dodge it.

Understanding Different Behavior Styles

Great communicators know that people are all different. They think, act, make decisions, and see the world in their own individual ways. With excellent social skills you can identify how people want to communicate and then change your natural style to fit theirs.

Notice the following model. It can help you understand the uniqueness of individuals, and what to do to communicate with them.

Behavior Styles Model

Talkers are outgoing, friendly, affable people. They like people, are colorful, and are fun to be with. They're easy to approach and talk to. They buy from people they like. They often find making decisions difficult because they don't like to reject or disappoint people—even salespeople. They need social approval and acceptance, and their greatest fear is the loss of it.

Doers are bottom-line, get-it-done people. They're pressed-for-time, action-oriented, decisive people who want to deal with the "top person." They make quick decisions once they think they have a grasp of the facts. They crave respect for their achievements. Their greatest fear is the loss of power.

Controllers are reserved and distant. They're logical and unemotional. They want facts and accurate information, and aren't swayed by your enthusiasm and personality—they may even be turned off by it. They're very analytical and well organized and will make decisions only after carefully digesting all the facts and data. Their greatest fear is being wrong.

Supporters are easygoing, steady, dependable, and loyal. They want to go slow and get a lot of information. They're detail-minded and don't make quick decisions. They usually prefer to work in the background rather than take center stage. They're team players. They need sameness, predictability, and security. Their greatest fear is running risks.

As you review this model and the description of each style, please remember the following important points and you'll understand the model more completely:

1. No style should be considered better than another.
2. People are generally combinations of two styles, with one being dominant, the other secondary.
3. Usually the combinations are of contiguous styles. For example, a person could be a Talker/Doer or a Doer/Talker, a Doer/Controller or a Controller/Doer, etc.
4. More complex people are often combinations of three styles, with the third one consciously developed.
5. It takes a combination of all styles to make up a good team.
6. Salespeople tend to sell and communicate consistently with their natural style; consequently, they often unwittingly misunderstand and miscommunicate with people of other styles.
7. Rapport is achieved faster when you change your style to match other people's styles.
8. With practice, you can identify and match others' styles unconsciously.
9. Each style wants information presented in different ways and they naturally make decisions differently.
10. Your customers' motivations are largely colored by their behavior styles.

I realize that all this is far too much to process and remember simply by reading about it. But through repetition and daily practice, you'll make it part of your natural skills.

Once you've begun to intuitively blend your style with the people with whom you're communicating, you'll be amazed how much it helps you sell more.

Let's think about some clues that will help you identify each style—remembering that people are combinations of either two or occasionally three styles.

Talkers talk about people—relationships, family, friends. They're more interested in what *they* talk about than what *you* say. They generally aren't good listeners. Their minds can wander when you're talking, thinking about what they want to say when you pause for a breath of air. They don't process details well. They're bored easily with information that doesn't involve people. They're often indecisive.

Doers talk about results, getting things done, power, achievement. They want to tell you about themselves—their success, victories, ideas, experiences. They're often surrounded with power symbols—pictures of themselves with other high achievers. They don't like chitchat, but will usually have plenty of time to talk about "How I got where I am today." They exhibit restless, nervous mannerisms. They make quick decisions when convinced of bottom-line results.

Controllers are analytical, logical, and detail-oriented. They talk about standards, measurements, conditions, statistics. They're unemotional. They listen, remember, and retain facts well. They're not swayed by emotion or enthusiasm. They take time in decision making. They gather facts and digest them well; they can be cool and appear to be aloof. They're logic or reality-oriented, and not so much creative or idea thinkers. They have neat, organized environments.

Supporters are good listeners. They're loyal, conscientious, honest, salt-of-the-earth types. They're steady, dependable, punctual, and slow to make decisions. They're peacemakers, don't like conflict, need order, process, predictability. They like repetitive, redundant work activities. They are resistant to change and hang on to old, tried-and-true ideas, products, possessions. They're good team players. Supporters will usually show little initiative or creativity since they aren't results-oriented but do seek safety and security.

First understand your style, and your natural way of talking, listening or thinking. Then as you identify other people's styles, you can quickly see how you might communicate or miscommunicate with them.

As you use this knowledge of behavior styles you'll fill a very strong need that most people have—the need to be understood and valued.

HOW TO GAIN THE MOST FROM THIS CHAPTER

One of the deepest needs your customers have is to feel that you understand them. This bypasses logic and goes to the deepest emotional dimensions within us. Good communication takes place between you and your customers when you genuinely attempt to understand *who* they are, *how* they think, and *what* wants, needs, goals, or problems they want filled, satisfied, or solved. It's also important to know *why* they want them.

I suggested four Action Guides to practice to help you have effective communication with customers. They are:

1. Ask open-ended, indirect questions that draw out people's wants, needs, opinions, and feelings.
2. Listen without biases, distractions, or interruptions.
3. Understand what people say and why they say it.
4. Paraphrase your understanding back to customers and make sure they feel understood.

When you practice the ideas I've shared with you in this chapter, you'll answer one of the strongest, most motivating needs your customers have—the need to be understood and valued.

As a constant reminder, say this self-suggestion each day: "When I help people feel important and understood, they'll think I'm important and will want to understand me." Before long this will automatically trigger positive, customer-focused behaviors.

10 HELPING PEOPLE FEEL UNDERSTOOD

Assessment

Please take a few moments and check off the number that best describes your present beliefs, boundaries, or behaviors. Use these descriptors as guidelines.

5–Always true, without exception
4–Mostly true
3–True more often than not
2–True only part of the time
1–True only occasionally

1. I'm mainly focused on customers understanding my product.	5 4 3 2 1 | 1 2 3 4 5	1. I'm mainly focused on how well customers feel I understand them.
2. I want customers to buy from me; I don't care how they see me.	5 4 3 2 1 | 1 2 3 4 5	2. I want customers to see me as an extension of themselves.
3. My success is enhanced as my customers become more important to me.	5 4 3 2 1 | 1 2 3 4 5	3. My success is enhanced as I become more important to my customers.
4. I give attention to getting customers to know me.	5 4 3 2 1 | 1 2 3 4 5	4. I give attention to getting to know my customers.
5. I believe that customers are purely motivated by logic and my product features.	5 4 3 2 1 | 1 2 3 4 5	5. I understand that customers are often motivated more by emotions than logic.
6. My customers are most interested in getting the best price; relationships have little to do with their buying decisions.	5 4 3 2 1 | 1 2 3 4 5	6. My customers are most interested in the value I can create for them.

	5 4 3 2 1	1 2 3 4 5	
7. How much I talk and listen never really dawns on me.	5 4 3 2 1	1 2 3 4 5	7. I'm very conscious about how much time I talk and listen in my contacts with customers.
8. I'm so busy talking to customers that I don't listen all that much.	5 4 3 2 1	1 2 3 4 5	8. I'm so busy listening to customers, that I don't talk that much.
9. I'm always concerned about telling my customers as much as I can about my products.	5 4 3 2 1	1 2 3 4 5	9. I'm always concerned about customers knowing I care about them and their needs.
10. I never think about changing my style to fit my customers' styles.	5 4 3 2 1	1 2 3 4 5	10. I consciously try to change my natural style and adapt to each customer's style.

- Add up the numbers in the right-hand column. _____
- Add up the numbers in the left-hand column. _____
- Subtract the left-hand column total from the right-hand column total and score yourself. _____

Assessments scoring guide is on page 35.

Keeping Score—Chapter 10

Behavior that gets evaluated, gets improved.

On a scale of 1–10, please evaluate your performance of each of these Action Guides.

	S	M	T	W	T	F	S
1. I asked open-ended, direct questions that drew out people's wants, needs, opinions, and feelings.							
2. I listened without biases, distractions, or interruptions.							
3. I understood what people said and why they said it.							
4. I paraphrased my understanding back to customers and made sure they felt understood.							
Total Each Day							

11 Self-Talk

Choosing What to Say When You Talk to Yourself

KELLY FOREHAND HAS BEEN AN INSPIRATION TO ME SINCE he first came to work in our office over twenty-five years ago. His positive, cheery self-talk, in the midst of incredible adversity, has helped him succeed beyond the level of most people who have no disabilities.

It all started when he was in high school. His chief aim was to play professional football and then become a stockbroker. But one night in a football game he was hit from behind, and lay motionless on the grass. Unable to even breathe, he wondered if he was already dead or still alive.

His spinal cord was severed and quickly an emergency crew arrived and got him breathing again. As Kelly lay in a rehab hospital for several weeks he was faced with the possibility that he'd never walk again; he'd certainly never play professional football.

After going through the cycle of denial, anger, depression, and acceptance, he made the decision that his disability would not keep him from his other goal of becoming a stockbroker.

Despite his quadriplegic condition, he finished high school and graduated from college with a BBA degree. His dream was to go with Merrill Lynch, but when he applied he was told that they didn't hire anyone under twenty-five years old.

Facing the possibility that they were really saying, "We don't think a person with your disability could make it here," he said, "Okay, I'll come back when I'm twenty-five."

While in college he had married, gotten a van fitted for his handicap, and had taken one of my personal development courses. So after Merrill Lynch's rejection, he came to me and asked for a job. He was very honest in telling me that he planned to be a broker, and was not looking for a long-term job.

Sure enough, when Kelly turned twenty-five he camped out at Merrill Lynch's door, and was hired as a broker. He did well for years, was promoted to manager, and eventually became a regional manager of several offices.

Today, Kelly serves as a senior vice president and head of the trust department of a bank.

Knowing him all these years, I was always intrigued by his positive attitude. But, digging deeper, it was really how he chose to talk to himself. Always cheerful, with a constant smile on his face, he had learned to talk to himself in positive ways.

I asked him one time how he stayed so cheerful. He put on his usual smile and told me about being in the rehab hospital after the accident, getting over his "pity party," and realizing that he had a choice how he would live his life.

He took me through his thought process. He accepted the fact he was a quadriplegic, and would possibly remain that way throughout his life. He told himself that he could live on a small disability income, and vegetate, or he could go on with his life plans, minus the pro football career. He reasoned that while he couldn't walk, his mind was as good as ever.

That day he made a decision to go on with his life plans.

He chose to talk to himself in a way that would lead him to success in his chosen field. He still does.

Pessimists and Optimists

Each of us basically chooses one of two ways to look at life.

- Positively—choosing to focus on its opportunities, blessings, and possibilities
- Negatively—choosing to focus on its problems, limitations, and challenges

Positive, or optimistic people tend to view life as presenting unfolding opportunities. They tend to see bad circumstances as temporary obstacles to work through to get to the rewards they believe lie ahead.

Negative, pessimistic people tend to think that bad events will last a long time, and will keep them from reaching creative goals.

In his book, *Learned Optimism*, Martin E. P. Seligman draws a clear distinction between these two personality types.

> The defining characteristics of pessimists is that they tend to believe bad events will last a long time, will undermine everything they do, and are their fault. The optimists who are confronted with the same hard knocks of this world, think about misfortune in the opposite way.

He goes on about optimists,

> They tend to believe defeat is a temporary setback, that its causes are confined to this case. The optimists believe defeat is not their fault. Circumstances, bad luck, or other people brought it about. Such people are unfazed by defeat. Confronted by a bad situation, they perceive it as a challenge and try harder.

In all these cases, choices were made that influence our sales in several ways.

Projections

Any serious student of human behavior has long observed that we tend to project our own beliefs, attitudes, and moods on to others. Customers intuitively feel these in salespeople who contact them. A person's body language, facial expressions, placement of eyes and hands—these are subliminally communicated to customers.

Our own self-talk, which we think is contained within ourselves, is in fact broadcast through the channels just mentioned. Our own self-images—originally developed by our self-talk, and then the perpetuators of it—silently reveal themselves to those with whom we communicate.

This is only one way that our choices reveal themselves.

We Predict Our Future

Here's the principle: *What we repeatedly tell ourselves, we eventually believe.* On the flip side, *What we believe, we repeatedly tell ourselves.*

These are profound truths that you can prove to yourself by examining your self-talk, and projecting it on the screen of your recent life circumstances. Your current sales, income, client level, and life circumstances are manifestations of your inner beliefs, which are the result of your past self-talk.

Self-talk is what we tell ourselves about who we are, what our possibilities are, how we interpret circumstances, how we deal with difficulties. These are major determining factors of whether we enjoy success or failure in selling.

I've observed over and over how salespeople's *views of selling,* and their *views of their possibilities,* heavily impact their success. When people view selling as identifying needs and creating value for customers above the price they charge them, an amazing transformation takes place within them. Paradoxically, when they view themselves as helping others, their self-esteem is enhanced.

On the opposite end of the spectrum, when salespeople only focus on the sale and their rewards of making it, much of their enthusiasm and personal pride vaporizes.

Since we're body, mind, and soul—holistic beings—when one part of us is affected, the whole system is eventually influenced. With this in mind, Seligman suggests that:

- Optimists catch fewer infectious diseases than pessimists do.
- Optimists have better health habits than pessimists.
- Evidence suggests that optimists live longer than pessimists.

As you'll see in this chapter, you have the choice of what level of thinking you demonstrate, and you have the ability to choose your future by selecting the views that usher in your life circumstances.

How you explain circumstances to yourself often changes your future events.

Resilience in the Face of Rejection

If you're an average salesperson, you probably experience much more rejection than acceptance. Unless you're a highly seasoned veteran with an established clientele, you probably attempt to make more sales than you actually close. How do you handle this?

Your emotional resilience becomes a necessary trait for a sustained successful sales career. The following purposes, or beliefs, contrast positive ones with negative ones. Choosing and applying the right ones will help you move past negative situations, defeats, and disappointments that stop many other salespeople.

CREATIVE	DESTRUCTIVE
"I'm here to help you if I can."	"I'm here to sell you something if I can."
"I view your decision as being whether or not you need what I have."	"I view your decision as accepting or rejecting me as a person."
"I take obstacles in stride."	"Rejection and missed sales cause me to become discouraged."
"I focus on the benefits I can help my customers enjoy."	"I focus on getting my customers to buy from me."
"I look at mistakes as learning experiences."	"I look at mistakes as reasons why I'm not cut out for selling."
"I view defeats as temporary."	"I view defeats as reasons to quit."

Whether we're emotionally resilient or we quit in the face of defeats and adversity, determines our long-term success in selling. I'm convinced that it's the degree of our emotional tensile strength that keeps us in the game over the long haul.

It's easy to say destructive statements to ourselves when we fail. We often explain them away with words like "I'm just not cut out to be a salesman." Or "The door is permanently closed at the XYZ company." Or " I just can't handle the uncertainty of selling."

Take a few moments and remember what you've automatically said to yourself when you've been rejected. In fact, pick out two or three recent times you've been turned down, lost a sale, or an account. How did you explain these circumstances to yourself? How did you explain them to others?

As you recall your explanation to yourself or others when these situations happened you'll see that you fell somewhere between the optimistic and pessimistic ends of the scale.

Take a look at the following "explanations," and then come back and rethink your two or three situations.

OPTIMIST'S EXPLANATIONS FOR DEFEAT

"They didn't need our product or service at this time."

"Their budget didn't allow them to purchase at this time."

"It's a timing issue for them."

"I need to spend more time in understanding their situation."

"They didn't fully understand my solutions."

"I never got to see the real decision makers."

PESSIMIST'S EXPLANATION FOR DEFEAT

"I'm not a good salesperson."

"They didn't like me."

"I didn't want to be too pushy."

"I didn't really think they'd buy from me."

"I didn't communicate well with them."

"The sale was bigger than I could have handled anyway."

After reading these explanations of defeat, go on to read the following ways we can explain success.

OPTIMIST'S EXPLANATION OF SUCCESS

"I prepared well and expected to close the sale."

"I had total confidence that our product or service would fill their needs."

"I proved my case and expected the decision makers to trust me."

"I felt good about helping create value for this customer."

"I look forward to following up from time to time."

"I feel worthy of being compensated consistently with the value I help create."

PESSIMIST'S EXPLANATION OF SUCCESS

"I wasn't sure whether they'd buy from me or not."

"I hope our product or service will satisfy my customer."

"I was very uneasy about how I could relate to the decision makers."

"I was afraid that I couldn't make the sale."

"I'm reluctant to follow up, because they may be unhappy."

"I hope they don't think I'm just doing this so I can make money off them."

Okay, this is a pivotal learning moment. Stop reading, go back, and review the explanations for success or defeat. Reflect back to some of your own experiences when you succeeded or were rejected. Relate your responses, self- talk, or explanations after each of these experiences.

Knowing what you now know, if you could replay your responses to those experiences, what would you tell yourself now?

Successful Salespeople

Successful salespeople are different than most other people. I've observed thousands of successful salespeople, and a common trait I see in them is that they tend to believe what they want to believe. We generally believe that our best days are ahead. We also fantasize a lot. We dream about rewards. In a sense, we tend to distort reality at times. We believe that the next success is right around the corner. We think that everyone should be as excited about our product or service as we are. We wake up in the morning visualizing having just made the big sale.

Are you like other people? No!

No, successful salespeople aren't like other successful people. But there are in fact many people who *need* a certain level of pessimism or skepticism to do their jobs well. I can't imagine a police officer asking a criminal how he can create value for him.

In a sense many highly successful salespeople distort reality. The reality may be they lost a big sale; but their distorted view was that their prospect just didn't understand them, and they'll close the next opportunity.

When I think of this type of person I am reminded of a college football team I once worked with. The quarterback was a true "salesman" in his responses to adversity. Whenever he got creamed by an opponent, he'd jump up, plant a big smile on his face, go into the huddle, and laugh about how they were going to score on the next play.

I used to laugh and tell him that he was so optimistic that whenever he threw an interception, he celebrated because he just knew this would cause the opponents to become complacent.

Now, there was a salesperson!

Let the Mirror Talk Back to You

One of our course participants shared his example of how he used self-talk to build new beliefs over time. As soon as he enters his bathroom each morning and evening he looks into the mirror and the person in it says to him, "Well, hello! What do you do?"

"I'm a professional salesperson," he responds.

"Oh, really? What makes you professional?"

"I get to know people, find out if they have needs I can help them fill, or problems I can help them solve. If they do, I find out what they are, and honestly decide if I have the right stuff for them."

"What if they don't have needs they want filled?"

"Then I congratulate them, and ask to stay in touch with them."

"What if you can't sell them anything?"

"That's okay. There are plenty of people who need my help. All I have to do is to see who needs me, and who doesn't."

"You really sell stuff like this?"

"Absolutely. Not only do I sell stuff this way but when I adopted this view of selling I almost doubled my sales."

"Well I compliment you," the person in the mirror says. "Are you kidding me, or do you really sell more this way?"

"Yes, I do. And my customers like to buy this way. I develop loyal customers who trust me, because they know that I'm there to help them, not just to sell them."

"Wow," the person said. "I'll bet you really feel good about selling this way."

"Not only do I feel good selling this way, but my customers feel good about it."

What a great conversation with the "man in the mirror." And powerful, too. Especially when you're looking into the right eyeball of the person in the mirror, and can feel his or her emotions.

Why not try it and see what happens? See if it changes the way you think and talk to yourself.

From Self-Suggestion to Truth

Your current beliefs about your sales possibilities were once self-suggestions that you've accepted as the truth about yourself. You then act on what you believe to be the truth about your abilities and possibilities. Your perception of the truth about you is embedded in the deep programming in your "I Am." Whatever this perception is, whether it's true or untrue, your actions, feelings, behavior, and abilities are consistent with it.

When you first begin conscious self-suggestions, you'll probably find resistance between these conscious suggestions and your unconscious beliefs. This is normal. Expect it.

Initially, it's important that you don't succumb to *logic* and *truth*. Those tell you that what you're affirming isn't a reality. Of course it isn't—at that time. It will only become your truth as you continually talk to yourself about what you want to become, and do it with feeling. You'll eventually emotionally buy whatever you repeatedly tell yourself.

So the question becomes, "How do you get the heavy doors of your deeply held self-beliefs to open up and accept new, expanded truths?"

Carefully read the following ways to develop new expanded self-beliefs.

Emotionalize Your Conscious Self-Suggestions

Logic doesn't reach and change inner beliefs as powerfully as emotions do. Think of how sudden traumatic experiences have left certain memo-

ries deep within you, and how those old tapes occasionally replay themselves in your mind. We do this when we recall old failures.

Here are some suggestions for emotionalizing your self-talk:

1. Design a specific statement that describes a new attitude or belief
   that you'd like to have.
2. Define the highest reward you'll enjoy when you program this new
   belief within your "I Am."
3. Write these statements on a card, carry it with you, and repeat them
   to yourself several times each day.
4. Visualize the reward you'll enjoy when this new attitude or belief is
   so fixed in your "I Am."

It's your emotionalized gratification, or hope of reward, that will in
time penetrate the walls that have surrounded your inner beliefs. The
intensity of your excitement will be the measure of your results.

Equate Your New Goals with Old Accepted Truths

Another way to accelerate the reprogramming of old beliefs into higher
ones is to equate them with your already accepted "truths" about yourself.

Here's how you can do this.

1. Design a specific statement that describes a new goal, attitude,
   belief, skill, or level of performance.
2. Think of a time in your life when you were successful reaching a
   similar goal; write down what happened.
3. Write a statement on a card that essentially says, "If I did that, then
   I can do this now!"
4. Follow through by saying this statement several times each day.
   Each time you say it, end your statement by saying "and that's the
   truth!"

The principle here is that our "I Am" only accepts ideas, suggestions,
or new goals that it perceives to be the truth about ourselves, or are consistent with our previous actions.

I've used this principle many times in my own selling. I remember the largest sale that I and an associate ever made. We had called on the director of education and training at Chevrolet a couple of times. We had received a warm reception but hadn't gotten close to a sale. It was a bit intimidating to think that an organization our size could actually help one as big as Chevrolet.

Then it dawned on me that I had worked with a number of car dealers a few years earlier, and had helped them increase sales, salesperson retention, and customer satisfaction ratings. So, I said to myself, "If I helped these dealers increase their sales and profitability then, we can help many more now."

I kept saying this to myself.

It just so happened that the education and training director, Lou Elbert, had known about dealerships that I had worked with in the past years. I asked him to recall the results they had enjoyed back then. He remembered them and was very positive about the results the dealers had enjoyed.

It was a while before we closed the sale, eventually installing our Integrity Selling process in 900 Chevrolet dealerships, with 26,000 people going through it the first year.

I'm sure that the daunting size of Chevrolet would have made me doubt we could help them if I had not kept saying, "If I helped those dealers (a few years ago) increase their sales and profitability then, we can help many more now."

A new, larger belief was accepted when I compared it with a previously proven and accepted truth.

Self-Talk Distinguished from Self-Suggestion

Self-talk is what we unconsciously say to ourselves when we have life experiences—when we have successes, defeats, good times, bad times. When we set higher goals, attempt to call on higher level decision makers, or make larger sales. When we face decisions, problems, or situations with people. It's how we explain our actions, feelings, and behavior to ourselves.

Coming from deep within us are messages, delivered through hunches, intuition, or feelings that say to us:

"I'm capable of that."

"I'm not capable of that."

"I deserve that."

"I don't deserve that."

"That's possible for me to do."

"That's not possible for me to do."

Our self-talk is largely automatic. Again, it's not based on truth, but what we *perceive* to be the truth. When at our "I Think" level we say, think, decide, or commit to something, the programming in our "I Am" immediately assesses it against old accepted parameters, and either agrees or disagrees with the new statement through *self-talk*.

Most of the time the beliefs in our "I Am" will either overrule or approve the choices or actions of our "I Think." The approval or over-ruling will come dressed as hunches, fears, intuition, or other emotions sent up through our "I Feel."

Self-suggestions are conscious statements or wishes that we choose with our "I Think," and say to ourselves with repetition, over a period of time. By this process these suggestions can eventually reach our "I Am" dimension and become new beliefs.

New beliefs then produce new self-talk, and new self-talk eventually causes new inner beliefs. They work together.

You can accelerate these self-suggestions being translated into deep beliefs when you:

- Emotionalize them.
- Perceive them to be consistent with other accepted "truths" about yourself.

Let me emphasize this universal truth: what we feed our minds, we eventually become. And then what we become produces our self-talk.

The Role of Discipline

When most of us think of discipline, we think of denial, toughing it out, or making ourselves do what we don't want to do.

Let's understand that our behaviors or actions are mostly motivated by emotions, not logic or discipline. On average, our actions are motivated 15 percent by logic or discipline, and 85 percent by emotions or feelings. Or, said another way, when our emotions and our conscious willpower are in conflict, our emotions will win around 85 percent of the time.

Highly effective people have learned to use discipline—not to change behavior, but to do deep programming that helps them develop new self-beliefs. They know that these new beliefs will then influence their external behaviors. They know to use willpower to do certain learning and mind-conditioning activities like self-suggestion, and then leave it up to their marvelous Creative Mechanism to bring forth results in changed automatic behaviors.

For example, instead of using discipline to force yourself to have a high activity level, use it to program the following beliefs deep within your "I Am."

- "Selling is creating value for customers."
- "I want to help as many people as I can."
- "I know that I'll be rewarded consistently with the level of value I create for the most people."
- "I deserve to enjoy higher levels of success when I help more people."

When these beliefs or values are programmed within you, you'll *want* to make more calls, rather than dreading or avoiding them. The more you use discipline to make more calls, the more likely it is that you increase your dread and avoidant behaviors.

Let's think of another way to help you.

Create Creative Tension

Higher success, personal growth, or enjoying more of life's rewards almost always involves consciously causing *creative tension* within yourself. You do this by developing the desire to reach higher, healthier, success goals that are greater than the ones you're currently enjoying.

When there's a gap between where you are now and where you'd like to be, a tension is created depending on your desire level. Also, as you seriously consider reaching higher goals, a natural tension builds within you.

Negative conflict is triggered when the safety of our current comfortable behaviors is threatened by new goals, because of the changes we'll have to make. Positive conflict is created when we focus on the rewards and gratification that new goals will bring us, and have a strong desire for them.

Our attitude, focus, or viewpoint becomes the determinant of whether the created conflict is positive or negative.

We trigger a natural tension when we set new goals, either positively or negatively. When we focus on the rewards of reaching new goals, we fuel our enthusiasm and new energies. It gives us "go-power." But focusing on the difficulties of reaching the new goals weakens us. It causes us to retreat back to a tensionless, comfortable level.

When we set new goals, we often begin to ask such questions as "Is this possible?" "What if I expend all this effort and I don't reach the goals?" "What if I try and fail?"

It's at this point that you must counter with self-talk: "Of course this goal is possible." "When I expend effort, something good will happen." "I can only fail by not trying." Identify and argue with your negative self-talk. Don't allow it to express itself unchallenged.

Expect internal tension, anxiety, or concern whenever you set new goals. Immediately focus on the rewards and gratification you'll enjoy, rather than the roadblocks or possible difficulties of reaching them.

HOW TO GAIN THE MOST FROM THIS CHAPTER

We all engage in self-talk daily as we go about dealing with challenges, working on new goals, facing problems, or other life events. This automatic self-talk is passing judgment on what we think we can do and what we think we can't do.

Please remember these two principles:

- What we repeatedly tell ourselves, we eventually believe.
- What we believe, we repeatedly tell ourselves.

Successful salespeople are generally different from other people. They tend to believe what they want to believe. They tend to see road-blocks and defeats as temporary. They tend, no matter how big their problems, to see light at the end of the tunnel. Others see the headlights of an oncoming locomotive.

I've learned that repetitive self-suggestions can help build new beliefs, which then produce new self-talk. I gave you these two ways to build new, inner beliefs, thus changing your beliefs that produce your self-talk.

1. Emotionalize your self-suggestions.
2. Equate your new goals with your old accepted truths or actual successful experiences.

Please reflect on the goals you've set. Answer the question, "What new self-beliefs will I need to develop to reach these goals?" Then begin to program these desired new beliefs into your "I Am," using self-suggestions. As this happens, these beliefs will then trigger positive, automatic self-talk.

Remember, your self-talk largely predicts your future. What you feed your mind, you'll eventually become.

Your self-suggestion this week is "What feed my mind, I become!"

11 CHOOSING WHAT TO SAY WHEN YOU TALK
     TO YOURSELF

Assessment

Please take a few moments and check off the number that best describes your present beliefs, boundaries, or behaviors. Use these descriptors as guidelines.

  5–Always true, without exception
  4–Mostly true
  3–True more often than not
  2–True only part of the time
  1–True only occasionally

1. I've never paid attention to my self-talk.	5 4 3 2 1 | 1 2 3 4 5	1. I'm well aware of my self-talk.
2. I tend to react to my self-talk.	5 4 3 2 1 | 1 2 3 4 5	2. I carefully choose my self-talk.
3. I tend to be stopped by defeats and disappointments.	5 4 3 2 1 | 1 2 3 4 5	3. I'm able to work through roadblocks.
4. I tend to think that bad events will last a long time.	5 4 3 2 1 | 1 2 3 4 5	4. I tend to think that bad events will soon pass.
5. I tend to beat myself up when I fail to make a sale.	5 4 3 2 1 | 1 2 3 4 5	5. I tend to use failed sales attempts as challenges to go on to the next one.
6. I don't believe that self-suggestion will really help me reach new goals.	5 4 3 2 1 | 1 2 3 4 5	6. I constantly use self-suggestions to help me build belief in new goals.
7. When I feel doubt or inner tension about actually reaching my new goal, I get discouraged and often give up.	5 4 3 2 1 | 1 2 3 4 5	7. When I feel doubt or inner tension about reaching a new goal I immediately refocus my thinking.
8. When I set new goals I often worry about whether or not I can reach them.	5 4 3 2 1 | 1 2 3 4 5	8. When I set new goals I get excited about the rewards I'll enjoy when I reach them.
9. I fail to reach most of the goals I set.	5 4 3 2 1 | 1 2 3 4 5	9. I reach most of the goals I set.
10. I don't really expect anything good to happen if I do the activities in this chapter.	5 4 3 2 1 | 1 2 3 4 5	10. I expect to enjoy high rewards from doing the activities of this chapter.

- Add up the numbers in the right-hand column. _____
- Add up the numbers in the left-hand column. _____
- Subtract the left-hand column total from the right-hand column total and score yourself. _____

Assessments scoring guide is on page 35.

Keeping Score—Chapter 11

Behavior that gets evaluated, gets improved.

On a scale of 1–10, please evaluate your performance of each of these parts of the Breakthrough Process.

	S	M	T	W	T	F	S
1. I examined my self-talk today.							
2. I thought about a new goal, skill, or performance level, and the inner beliefs that I need to have to bring them about.							
3. I repeated this week's self-suggestion today.							
4. I compared my self-beliefs against those listed as creative or destructive.							
5. I followed the four steps of emotionalizing my self-suggestions.							
Total Each Day							

12 **Purpose**

Finding Meaning in What You Do

"UNTIL THOUGHT IS LINKED WITH PURPOSE THERE IS NO intelligent accomplishment," wrote James Allen in *As a Man Thinketh*. Thought linked with purpose brings its possessor power, energy, and meaning.

Consider my old friend Bill Johnson, whom I've known since our college days. A person with impeccable integrity, Bill has always sold things out of a sense of purpose. For years he was highly successful selling investment products to banks and high net worth individuals. He was driven by a purpose to help others. One way he did this was by giving 20 percent of his income to his church.

This discipline, and all its accompanying side benefits, come back to serve him over and over. I've seen him suffer setback after setback, only to be so motivated by his purpose that he had the emotional and spiritual stamina to move through them to enjoy even higher levels of achievement.

Three years ago, he was diagnosed with twenty tumors in his liver and one in his pancreas. He was given three to six months to live.

Always scoping around for business deals, he came across the opportunity to build a dairy, with the help of a seasoned veteran in that business. It would mean that they would have to borrow $10 million.

After talking to his son, Jim, he asked his wife, Sue, "You know that I'm a short-timer with a few months to live. Do you want me to borrow $10 million to build a dairy?"

Sue asked him, "How much do we owe now?"

"About a million dollars," he replied.

She said, "I can't see much difference in owing one million or ten million. I couldn't pay either one. And who knows, this challenge may get you out of bed each morning and be good for you."

Bank of America lent Bill, his son, and the new experienced partner the money.

Before that time Bill had dropped from 205 pounds to 168, and the cancer left him with no energy. But after the dairy was started, he got up each morning, drove over 100 miles, and back home that night. The doctors at M. D. Anderson Hospital in Houston put him on Sandostatin, and he took it every two weeks.

I had dinner with Bill and Sue recently; his weight is up to 194 and he's feeling good. Their dairy milks 3,100 cows twice a day, and their first year's net income was over $2,000,000.

"How have you done all this?" I asked him.

"Having this project at a time I was very sick did get me out of bed each day and working on a program that was very exciting to me. The Lord has blessed us far beyond anything we ever dreamed of or even imagined. I'm so thankful for Sue, Jim, and my new partner. I'm especially grateful to Sue, as I was seventy years old facing a battle with cancer and she said, 'Let's do it.'"

Bill and his partners named the dairy *Milagro,* which in Spanish means "miracle."

"Thought allied with purpose becomes a creative force"—James Allen again.

Purpose Is the Why You Do What You Do

"He who has a *why* to live can bear almost any *how*" wrote German philosopher Friedrich Nietzsche.

Why do you do what you do? Why do you sell what you sell? What is the *why* of your life? What is your *purpose*?

As I've observed thousands of salespeople over the years, I've clearly seen a correlation between their success and what their conscious or unconscious purpose was. In simple terms, I've seen their purpose fall somewhere between the two extremes of their own survival on one hand, and their creating high value for customers on the other.

I've seen person after person fail because they could never get their focus on their customer and off their own financial or emotional survival. I know how tough this is to do, because I've been there. I can remember times when I was so concerned with paying bills and feeding my family that I was almost totally blinded to a higher reason why I did what I did.

A survival focus can force us into its small emotional prison cell, making us fight like crazy to get out. But it's in the fight that we can gain the strength of character to move forward. The will to fight through our struggles is fueled by the strength of our purpose.

Become a Realistic Dreamer

A realist often says, "Here's where I am, so here's where I am." They stay where they are. A dreamer might say, " I choose to live in this fantasy, and not take responsibility for my own success. A realistic dreamer says, "I am where I am today, but I don't have to be here tomorrow."

A better tomorrow begins with the adoption of a clear purpose—a statement that specifically defines why you do what you do—why you sell what you sell.

You can have several levels of purpose. Among them might be:

- Spiritual—a main reason for your years on this planet
- Family—a reason for your role as a father, mother, sister, or brother
- Career—a reason why you sell what you sell

There are other areas in which you'll want to define your purpose, but for the sake of this book, let's keep it on your sales career—with one caveat, that you understand that a spiritual and family purpose statement will strongly support and enhance your career purpose.

Your Purpose

Right now, and no matter what level of sales success you're enjoying or struggling with, please take a pad or a sheet of paper and write a statement of your career purpose. Here's an outline of what you might write out.

1. *My career purpose is to create as much value for as many customers as I can.*

2. *Here are specific ways I can help them.*

    a. _____

    b. _____

    c. _____

    d. _____

3. *I will end each day by writing down the names of customers that I will contact the next day.*
    a. *I will write down the specific value I can create for them.*
    b. *I will write down how they'll feel when I do.*
    c. *I will write down how I'll feel when I do.*

4. *I will read this at the close of each day, causing my creative "I Am" to work on it during the night when I'm asleep.*

Wherever you are in your sales career, you can do this exercise each day. If you're on a survival level, this will help you to move past it. If you're on a very high level of success, you'll also find great benefits from doing this mind-conditioning process.

Steve Znerold, agent for The Principal Financial Group in Des Moines, Iowa, is a great example of a high producer who's still open to learn. His commissions have been over $1 million each year for the past few years. Yet he's still an eager student. In such a refreshing way, he has told me several times how he's not helping as many people as he'd like to help.

Steve constantly challenges himself. I shared this four-step process with him a couple of years ago. He absorbed it with the hunger of the high achiever that he is. It was no surprise that his next year found him enjoying about a 20 percent increase in sales and income.

I've observed that he'll never learn everything he wants to learn, and will always be eager to serve his clients in higher ways.

A committed family man, Steve has a high achievement drive fostered and reinforced by his higher purpose.

Purpose Is Always Looking Outward

Here's the paradox: a purpose that's focused inward will never take you to the highest levels of sales success that you're capable of reaching. It just can't. Our Creator designed us to enjoy the greatest life meaning by serving others.

The more we serve and fill the needs of others, the more meaning we enjoy. Yes, a paradox—a seeming contradiction. Certainly it runs counter to our human, ego-focused nature. But truth it is.

Sales give us a great platform to serve others. As we view it with this purpose, we succeed.

Creative, healthy purpose can never be enjoyed by looking inward. Self-focus leads to loneliness, isolation, frustration, selfishness, and neurosis. It kills creativity and innovation. People who only focus on themselves live in very small, limited worlds. They can never expand beyond who and what they are. Often, and tragically, they get what they seek—themselves!

What most of us crave is a life filled with more meaning. Isn't that the silent stirring for which our souls cry out?

Purpose Gives Us a Reason for Growth

Energy, the will to achieve, the courage to try, fail, and succeed—these are all fueled and given motivation by purpose. It's the strength of our purpose that equips us to face risks and overcome obstacles and increase the degree of our success. All this involves growth and transcending our natural ego-driven human nature. Understanding this is the beginning of wisdom.

Human nature was revealed by the German philosopher Goethe, who said, "Everybody wants to be somebody; nobody wants to grow." The human condition is to stay where we are. Don't rock the boat. Don't launch out. Play it safe. Resist change and struggle. Go with the flow. Settle for where you are and what you have now. Don't challenge your boundaries. Draw back to a safe position when meeting problems or resistance.

That's what most people do. But not you!

You want to rise above the crowd and breathe the rarified air, free of the pollutants of limitations and run-of-the-mill. You want to enjoy what's freely waiting for you when you ascend to higher altitudes of thinking, spiritual growth, service, and self-fulfillment. And you'll make it if that's your deep desire.

The reason you've made it to this point is that you're ready to begin your Everest climb toward your own summit. Life has brought you to a base camp. You've been training and conditioning—experiencing struggles, failures, and difficulties in your life. You've grown through all these, and you know the climb ahead will require courage, stamina, and a will that won't be denied.

You're here because you've chosen to take responsibility for your quality of life. You've scaled smaller peaks in your life experience, thinking that that was what it was all about, only to stand on top of them, see still higher peaks in the distance, and say, *This still isn't all there is. There's more. I must keep climbing!*

You've had to throw off negative burdens, shut them out, put them behind you, and narrow your focus of resolve. You've had to move through the crowd of people who are content to paddle around in the kiddie pool of life. The very people who love to criticize the performance of others who have the courage to jump off the high diving board.

Maybe you've had to move away from people who would, in their need to control you, try to keep you down and prevent you from growing past them. This was very painful for you. At the time you questioned your values or your ethics or your spiritual beliefs, as other well-meaning and not-so-well-meaning people did. But you had to grow. You couldn't stand still and stifle, despite the pain.

In your journey, you've learned that the more you grow, the more you discover your capacity for growth. The more you've developed, the more you've manufactured potential for greater success. Your room for growth always expands as you walk further into it.

The size of the room for personal expansion becomes proportionate to the size of your desires, commitment, motivation, and thrill of the search.

But what drives you? What should drive you?

Personal Growth Must Have a Purpose

For optimum emotional and spiritual health, personal growth must be viewed as the *means* to a goal, not the goal itself.

When personal growth is a goal unto itself, it can easily become narcissism. This state of self-absorption and self-focus, then, insidiously inhibits our growth. In simple terms, the narcissistic person is more focused on the outer package than the inner being. If personal growth's aim is to "look good in a mirror," it can block us from developing, or even valuing, our inner spiritual essence.

I take issue with many of the personal growth processes, seminars, and movements of the last few decades. They led people into the wrong direction, preaching "nurture yourself." While there's certainly nothing wrong with doing that, it was the self-focus that led many into deeper ruts of low self-esteem. The more they struggled to find themselves, the more they sunk into the quicksand of self-absorption. Thus they actually lost themselves.

High self-esteem is invariably developed as a process of serving and creating value for others. Nurturing ourselves is an automatic benefit of nurturing others. We seem to receive the greatest rewards when we're not seeking rewards. I witness this over and over again in my development courses.

This cycle of growth—giving out and being reinforced—forms a healthy completeness. Both are necessary. To extend ourselves to others for the joy of doing it, and not for the expectation of rewards, is what sets off the reciprocity. Next, we must gracefully accept or receive the reciprocal reward that completes the cycle. It's a balance of freely giving and graciously receiving.

Here we often create imbalances. We may be selfishly focused on selling things for the sole reason of making money or enjoying recognition. We may even focus on creating value for customers and because of a feeling of unworthiness or codependence, deny ourselves the reciprocal blessing of receiving.

When my purpose of growth is to equip myself to create more value for others and when I then feel worthy to receive a reciprocal benefit, my "I Am" is nourished. A calm elegance is experienced. Understanding this need for balance brings us to specific actions, choices, thinking patterns, and strategies for attaining it.

Growth is from the inside out.

Strategies for Growing from the Inside Out

As we think of specific personal growth strategies, let's count the costs and compare them to the ultimate value we receive. This process is necessary to trigger our motivation to act. Setting new goals almost always induces tension, stress, uncertainty, and struggle. All are necessary, though, for meaning and purpose, for living in rarified air.

Viktor Frankl, author of *Man's Search for Meaning*, wrote much on the subject of growth:

> To be sure, man's search for meaning may arouse inner tension rather than inner equilibrium. However, such tension is an indispensable prerequisite for mental health. There's nothing in the world I venture to say that would so effectively help one to survive even the worst conditions as the knowledge that there is a meaning in one's life.

It was out of defeat and desperation that I found my own purpose. For six years I had owned a small furniture and interior design business and had planned to stay in it forever. That was until an economic downturn happened in our city, causing many businesses to close up or go broke.

I was in denial for a while. My payables became sixty to ninety days behind. Cash flow and sales were cut in half. Finally, I accepted the fact that there was no way to make it. Desperate, I visited my friend and minister, Joe Barnett. He convinced me that I could design a leadership course and conduct it at church.

That was the last thing in the world that I ever thought I could do, but because of my respect and admiration for Joe, I consented to do it. And in doing so, I discovered that I *could*, in fact, do it. That was my beginning.

When I first started I was permitted to get a quick glimpse of my purpose. It happened early one Saturday morning, as I was liquidating my store. I got there before anyone else, made a pot of coffee, sat down, and soberly stared into an almost surreal future. It was the closest thing to an epiphany I've ever experienced. It was like God said to me, "Okay, I'm going to show you what's going to happen. But look quickly, because this is the only time I'm going to be this clear and direct."

From that moment I clearly knew what I should do with the rest of my life and never doubted that I would touch the lives of many people. I didn't hear voices or see visions. I suddenly just knew, from the deepest part of me, that something special was happening.

Realizing that God must have a sense of humor, I've often said back to Him, "Yeah, well thanks for that snapshot. But why didn't You also tell me how many struggles I'd have? I had no idea it would be this difficult!"

The thrill of seeing people grow, change, discover, develop, and become is indescribable. It transcends just doing a job or earning money or even enjoying personal recognition. (Although all those things are nice.)

Over the last forty years, I've received many letters from our course participants and graduates telling of the benefits they've enjoyed. Knowing that lives are being touched in companies and organizations around the world drives me. It keeps me learning, discovering things I need to learn, growing.

Not long ago I was a keynote speaker at a company's international sales convention. Many of the people had been in my courses. One person after another came up and told me how their lives had been affected.

One man told me of the death of a daughter two years previously, and how before my course, he had not wanted to live. A few months after completing my Managing Goal Achievement course, he'd lost thirty pounds, bought a whole new wardrobe, and had seen his business take off.

Another person came up and told me that her sales had increased 430 percent since my course. Another told me of a reconciled marriage. This kind of encounter is a great experience that has happened many times over the years. Not only does it remind me of my purpose, but it converts all the necessary struggles into creative, exhilarating experiences. Without the struggles, my purpose wouldn't be as meaningful.

Accepting Responsibility for Growth

Growth and maturity travel the same road together. Maturity is expressed by accepting responsibility for our direction and goals, as well as problems and success levels. Most failure, emotional illness, and accompanying low self-esteem result from the avoidance of responsibility.

It's here that integrity—or the integration of your conscious and unconscious—becomes a factor. Remember that success is in the convergence of the actions, decisions, and choices of your "I Think" with the values, guiding principles, and knowledge of truth in your "I Am."

If, for instance, your "I Am" doesn't have beliefs or values that are congruent with your conscious choices, you'll torpedo yourself, create stress, or suffer internal conflicts. The creation of strong, positive emotions in your "I Feel" comes by having congruence between your "I Think" and your "I Feel." This positive convergence helps you release energy and moves you toward your goals.

So you can see that, working together, all three dimensions yield success, peace of mind, energy, enthusiasm, and confidence.

If, for instance, there was no conscious choice of direction, even positive values and beliefs in your "I Am" would have nowhere to take you. All dressed up, but no place to go. If there was a choice of direction in your "I Think," but it interacted with negative values or beliefs in your "I Am," only failure and frustration would occur. A place to go, but nothing to wear to the party.

You may not feel you've found your purpose yet. Let's think about that. Have you set goals, taken responsibility for reaching them, or committed to action? Are your supporting values, self-trust, view of your possibilities, or self-value consistent?

The following factors are the main determinants of your success and achievement.

1. Your supporting values
2. Your level of self-trust
3. Your level of self-value
4. Your view of your own possibilities
5. Your view of your actual abilities
6. Your positive internal programming that expects and feels worthy of success and prosperity

Think about these internal drivers of success, and you'll see how we miss the boat in so much of our formal education. We propagate the myths that knowledge is power, that SAT tests measure a student's ability to succeed, that the regurgitation of facts, figures, or dates constitutes an education, and that product knowledge equips you to sell successfully. But these factors, while necessary, don't in and of themselves guarantee success.

Success in life is based much more on *who* we believe we are than on *what* we know. Factors like limiting beliefs, weak values, and lack of purpose and goals keep many people from succeeding; it's often not lack of knowledge.

We've seen that when salespeople go out just to sell something, a conflict is internally created within them that will either guarantee failure or, at best, cause lower levels of success. When this purpose is to just "make a sale," it creates a *cognitive dissonance,* an internal conflict that then inhibits their performance.

I've seen many people fail in selling because they viewed it as doing something *to* people, rather than *for* them. In many cases this was exacerbated by their managers' demanding that they hit numbers and produce sales. While all salespeople have to hit their quotas, we've found that they hit much higher sales numbers when they focus on filling people's needs and creating the most value for them.

When salespeople's goals are to identify needs and create high value for clients, they transcend the need to sell something. They develop stronger trust and rapport with customers and increase their own self-respect and confidence. They invariably sell more.

Their actions reveal their purpose.

The Power of Purpose

If there's one thing I've learned from my own experiences, as well as the hundreds of thousands of people who have been in my courses, it's simply this: if the purpose—the goal, the choice, the decision, the direction—is right, there's almost always a way to reach it.

Doors mysteriously open when you bring sufficient definiteness of purpose. People, events, and forces seem to mysteriously give way to people with strong resolve.

When I liquidated my furniture and design business many years ago and began conducting leadership training courses, I initially knew that no one would pay to take the course until I could prove it was worthwhile and beneficial for them. So I committed to conduct courses with no compensation for one year in order to build up my own credibility.

Immediately I encountered a problem I hadn't anticipated.

I made those commitments assuming I'd have enough money to live on for a year. But when I finally closed out my business, leased out my building, and paid all of my bills, I had less than $1,000 left over to live on for a year. With a home mortgage, two car payments, two kids, and a wife, it appeared impossible. You can't make $1,000 stretch over all those costs.

But from the deepest part within me, I knew I'd find a way to make it. I didn't know how but I never doubted I would. Any possible difficulties were totally overshadowed by the incredible experience I had seeing people in my course grow.

As you can guess, it wasn't but a few milliseconds until the money was gone. The smallest bill became a problem, yet somehow they got paid. Twice that year I got income tax refunds in the mail, unsolicited and unapplied for. And it was always at the very last moment, when we had no money and no food in the house, and it seemed that we could go no further. I also got a check in the mail one day from a person who owed me some money that I'd completely forgotten about.

That'll get your attention.

The tough times for the next three years were completely eclipsed by the incredibly exhilarating experiences I was having seeing people's lives change each evening in my course sessions.

I was learning and growing and getting a picture of what I could become. This was so mind-blowing to me that it overpowered my struggles—leaving me with absolutely no doubt that my tough times were only temporary and would pay off big in the future.

While I learned that purpose opens doors, I also painfully learned that it's often the very last moment until they open—testing us, I suppose, to see if we're really committed, or if we're just playing it safe.

Purpose Gives Us a Vital Attitude

Another discovery I've made is that people who work through struggles and find higher success view their challenges differently than other people do.

Here's the discovery:

People who have strong purpose tend to view roadblocks as temporary.

Please read that again.

Yes, people who have strong purpose tend to view roadblocks as temporary; people with weak or no definite purpose tend to view them as permanent.

The two different attitudes are:

- "I'll work through this problem."
- "This problem is too tough for me to handle; I'll quit and do something else."

Almost without exception, high achievers view problems and struggles as temporary hurdles to jump over. Low achievers view them as impenetrable barriers that are too high to scale.

This is so true in selling, because it presents so many challenges and negative responses. We deal with rejection, uncertainty, disappointment, and then mix them with the thrill of the sale, of helping people, of enjoying their appreciation and respect. The question becomes, "Which do you give attention to and remember?"

How do we handle the highs and lows of selling? How we answer these questions with our actions and emotional responses determines our success level. Do you view problems and roadblocks as temporary or permanent? When you encounter them, as you always will, what's your natural response?

Fight or flight?

Few answers will determine your sales success more than this one.

I know of no better way for you to deal with your daily challenges than to be guided by your purpose! Spiritually, family-wise, and career-wise.

No one ever succeeds, whatever their calling, without definiteness of purpose.

HOW TO GAIN THE MOST FROM THIS CHAPTER

Purpose is the *why* you do what you do, *why* you sell what you sell. Your purpose can run the gamut between sheer survival and the need to create the most value for the most people.

As you read and review this chapter this week, please take just a few minutes and write your answers to the following mind-conditioning process. Take a notepad and write down your answers to the following statements.

1. *Tomorrow I will help the following people.*
2. *Here are specific ways I can help them.*
3. *Here's how they'll feel when I help them.*
4. *Here's how I'll feel when I help them.*

As you fill in your answer to these questions, write it out in longhand. Review it at the end of your day so your creative mechanism in your "I Am" dimension can process, plan, and prepare you for a great day tomorrow.

Let me warn you: your attempt to do this mentally will fail you, when compared to writing it out at the end of each workday. When you develop the habit of doing it, you'll want to continue, because of the success you'll experience. Regardless of your current success level you'll be blown away at how it helps you quickly increase your sales success, self-confidence, and strengthen your purpose.

Along with this you may want to say this self-suggestion: "I view challenges, set-backs, and roadblocks as temporary; there's always a way to get over them." Every time you encounter a problem, rejection, or a challenge of any kind or size, say it over to yourself several times.

Eventually, these practices will embed a strong sense of personal power and control within you. You'll learn that all problems are solvable if you keep trying, and this will serve you in many ways.

It's the strength of your purpose that will predetermine the level of your sales success. "He who has a *why* to live can always find a *how.*"

12 FINDING MEANING IN WHAT YOU DO

Assessment

Please take a few moments and check off the number that best describes your present beliefs, boundaries, or behaviors. Use these descriptors as guidelines.

5–Always true, without exception
4–Mostly true
3–True more often than not
2–True only part of the time
1–True only occasionally

1. Selling is just a way to make a living.	5 4 3 2 1 | 1 2 3 4 5	1. Selling gives me a chance to help people.
2. I'm not sure I'm cut out for selling.	5 4 3 2 1 | 1 2 3 4 5	2. Selling gives me a chance to use my talents.
3. My product or service is pretty much like my competitors'.	5 4 3 2 1 | 1 2 3 4 5	3. I'm excited about what my product or service does for people.
4. I'm uneasy about the economy or my marketplace.	5 4 3 2 1 | 1 2 3 4 5	4. I see great potential for my sales career.
5. I think about how I can make sales this month.	5 4 3 2 1 | 1 2 3 4 5	5. I think about how I can build a successful career.
6. I do not have a clear life purpose.	5 4 3 2 1 | 1 2 3 4 5	6. I have a clear life purpose.
7. When I set goals I do not think of a life purpose.	5 4 3 2 1 | 1 2 3 4 5	7. My goals are consistent with my life purpose.

8. Call reluctance and other emotional challenges seem to always hamper my ability to sell.	5 4 3 2 1	1 2 3 4 5	8. Knowing *why* I sell helps me work through fears and roadblocks.
9. I view problems as the reason why I can't sell more.	5 4 3 2 1	1 2 3 4 5	9. I view problems as something to work through.
10. I focus on what I can sell to people.	5 4 3 2 1	1 2 3 4 5	10. I focus on people I can help with what I sell them.

- Add up the numbers in the right-hand column. _____
- Add up the numbers in the left-hand column. _____
- Subtract the left-hand column total from the right-hand column total and score yourself. _____

Assessments scoring guide is on page 35.

Keeping Score—Chapter 12

Behavior that gets evaluated, gets improved.

On a scale of 1–10, please evaluate your performance of each of these parts of the Breakthrough Process.

	S	M	T	W	T	F	S
1. My career purpose is to create the most value for the most customers.							
2. I wrote down and reviewed specific ways I can help customers.							
3. I wrote down and reviewed how customers will feel when I help them.							
4. I wrote down and reviewed how I'll feel when I help customers.							
Total Each Day							

13 **Values**

Deciding What You Stand For

ALICE BAKER, A PERSON OF STRONG VALUES AND A GRAD-
uate of our Integrity Selling Course, was the manager of a real estate
office in Nashville, Tennessee. One of her friends called her one day and
told her about a man who was in the process of listing his $3.2 million
home with another Realtor. She explained to Alice that the man was a
busy attorney and wasn't sure he was making the right choice.

"Would you just do me a favor," Alice's friend asked, "and talk to him?
I don't think he'll list it with you, but you'd help him clear up some things
in his mind."

Alice gladly agreed to meet with the man.

In the meeting Alice quickly found out that the Realtors who had
talked to the man had all pushed pretty hard to sell him on listing his
home with them.

But Alice didn't work that way. In her initial contacts her attitude was,
"I'm not here to sell you on me; I'm here to help you make a choice of the
right agent for you."

The man told her that several agents had approached him. "They all
talked about how good they were, and how they'd market my home, and
no one really listened to me," he explained.

Alice asked him, "What would you expect from a Realtor that would
cause you to feel comfortable and serve you well?"

The man explained that he wanted someone who really loved his
home, and who understood all the quality he had originally built into it.
The people he'd talked to didn't seem to care. It just seemed like another
transaction to them.

Alice asked him to explain how he'd built the home. He showed her around for two hours—him talking, her listening. It was an eleven-thousand-square-foot home, and the man's son had just moved out, leaving much more room than he wanted to care for.

She asked him about some of the most memorable moments he'd had while living in it. Also, about how his friends and family had enjoyed it. She asked him how he wanted to communicate. He responded, "By e-mail. Don't call me, I'm too busy. I'll call you when I need you."

Alice asked him about other considerations, or thoughts, he had about selling his home.

She left him by saying, "If I can help you in any way, you call me."

The next day he called her and told her that he wanted her to list it.

"Why did you choose me?" she asked.

"Because you're the only one who listened to me; all the others wanted me to listen to them."

Alice Baker sells with strong, impeccable values. She has a servant's heart. She doesn't see selling as convincing, but rather as finding out what needs, goals, or objectives people have; then she decides whether or not she can help them.

Her sincerity, genuine listening skills, and honest desire to help others make her a very successful salesperson. People catch her enthusiasm and friendly spirit and want to do business with her.

"Who we are," Emerson wrote, "speaks so loudly that people can't hear what we say." He also wrote, "We pass for what we are. Character teaches above our wills."

Not only do we pass for what we are, but we also *sell* consistently with *who* we are. And it's our values that determine who we are.

We can't sell by one set of values and live by another. Our actions will ultimately reveal our true selves to ourselves and customers. Who we are is revealed by the real thoughts and values that motivate our actions.

Let's heed Emerson again: "A man passes for what he is worth. What he is engraves itself on his face, on his form, on his fortunes, in letters of light." He continues, "Concealment avails him nothing, boasting nothing. There is confession in the glances of his eyes, in his smiles, in salutations, and the grasp of hands." Then he makes the point, "Men know not why they do not trust him, but they do not trust him."

Yes, who you are impacts your sales success more than anything that you can learn about sales.

Your Values

Values are the rules by which you run your life. They form the boundaries of your behavior—moral and ethical lines in the sand that you'll not cross. Uncompromising standards that guide your decisions, actions, responses, and goals.

Your values are formed in the deepest parts of your "I Am" and are the best descriptors of who you are. While it is difficult to specifically describe what yours are, you reveal them in your actions and reactions to life situations. You developed them from the teaching you received, from models you see in people you love and respect, as well as those you don't love and respect.

I believe that we are naturally endowed with inherent abilities to distinguish right from wrong—unless our life experiences seal them off. We acquire certain inherent values as a spiritual birthright and then are given the opportunity to confirm or deny them in our choices, decisions, and life experiences.

People who truly listen to their spirit within, the Spirit of Wisdom, develop strong, positive values; most of us intuitively know what they are.

We care to listen to this inner voice when we ask questions like:

- *What is the truth?*
- *What is the right thing to do?*
- *What do I really need to use as a moral compass?*

To think about successful living—for your sales career and your life—and not explore the role of values in this journey would be to stop short of the real issues that drive your success.

Sooner or later in our intellectual, emotional, and spiritual growth, as well as our careers or daily lives, we come face-to-face with some significant questions:

- *What are my values?*
- *To what extent do they influence my sales success, goal achievement, and general level of personal fulfillment?*

- *What specific values will I need to follow in order to enjoy the enduring high level of success I desire to have?*
- *How strong is my commitment to follow the right course?*

Values on the Job

I once asked an audience of senior corporate executives, "How many of you would say that your most productive people are ones with strong, positive values?" Almost every hand went up.

Their near unanimous assent convinced me that at least most of them meant it. I've asked this question to dozens of audiences, and they all react the same positive way.

What could this possibly mean? Is there a connection between strong values and high productivity? Yes, I think there is. Especially as we frame it all in the context of enduring success.

In his bestselling *Good to Great,* Jim Collins's study of "Level 5 Leaders" found that the leaders of Fortune 500 companies who outperformed the stock market for fifteen years all shared some common personal ingredients. Among them were these:

1. Makes productive contributions through talent, knowledge, skills, and good work habits.
2. Contributes to the achievement of group's objective; works effectively with others in group settings.
3. Organizes people and resources toward the effective and efficient pursuit of predetermined objectives.
4. Catalyzes commitment to and vigorous pursuit of a clear and competing vision; stimulates the group to higher performance standards.
5. Builds enduring greatness through a paradoxical combination of personal humility plus professional will.

These common factors of highly successful corporate leaders indicate the existence of high values, ones that help create a positive, synergistic force to permeate organizations. You can translate the same points into sales leaders.

Do Honesty and Integrity Pay?

Let's get real. Do honesty and integrity pay? Look at history, where "Robber Barons" amassed huge wealth. Look at today, where people can defraud our government of millions in tax revenue, skip to Switzerland, make more millions doing who knows what, then be exonerated by a U.S. president. Apparently, dishonesty does pay for many people.

So is it really in your best interest to live by a strict moral code?

How about the commodity broker whose Park Avenue penthouse and yacht were purchased by cleaning out customers' investment accounts? Or the retail giant that underpays invoices and threatens to cut off supplies unless they credit them for the balance owed? Or the savings and loan titan who leaves investors with empty retirement accounts, who gets sent to a country club prison for two or three years, and then gets to live off his Swiss bank account for the rest of his life?

Does honesty really pay?

I think we must look at what "pay" is.

Is not being able to travel back to the United States good pay? Or does knowing what people think of you lead to personal contentment? Or does unconsciously knowing that I've breached ethical, moral, or other laws create internal conflict that prevents me from ever knowing true peace?

Can we break basic moral laws and be truly happy? Respected? Admired?

Each of us answers these questions with our choices and actions.

Life Tests Us

At many of life's intervals, as we face various situations, problems, opportunities or challenges, all of us have to make some basic decisions, such as:

How will I handle this?

Will I tell the truth when a half-truth might get me over the hump?

What are my ethical guidelines?

Will I focus on how much I can get or how much I can give?

Will I become a person whom others can trust?

Will I take shortcuts or will I build solid foundations for long-term success?

We make all of these choices. The sum of our choices then reveals our values, which go together to create our lives.

Our "I Am" is revealed.

Responsibility for Your Future

Choosing to take responsibility for the quality of life you want to enjoy is scary. It takes guts, and creates sober moments. It can leave you feeling very alone at times.

The truth is, choosing to take responsibility also brings zest to your life. It happens when you trade security blankets for parachutes. There are many tough decisions that must be made to enjoy successful living. You make many of these though often not realizing their full consequences until their effects are lived out. Wisdom is making the right choices and knowing that doing so will lead to long-term success.

It's here that your natural, decision-making, logical "I Think" must carry out the values intuitively steeped in your "I Am," and consciously choose to do what you know is right. Creating an inner congruence. Smoothing out internal conflicts that can subconsciously torpedo you. Valuing truth and integrity.

Many of the problems people have come on them because they make bad choices and take actions that compromise strong values. Then compounding them by attempting a cover-up.

Congruence is a choice we make. It's with our "I Think" that we consciously choose to do what we know in our hearts is right. Even when it might be more comfortable, cost less, and save face if we didn't.

Not long ago a man mashed in the front left fender of my car. I was doing some shopping for my daughters, and when I came out, parts of my left front fender and headlight were lying on the concrete.

"Oh man," I groaned angrily as I rounded the corner. "Would I ever like to get my hands on whoever did this!" I looked up at the windshield and saw a note that read, "I damaged your car. I have insurance. Call me at this number."

What an honest person. He obviously wanted to do what was right.

I called. He apologized, assured me that he was responsible, and gave me his insurance agent's name. It's hard to stay angry when someone does the right thing, especially when he could have just driven off or left me one of those notes that said, "I just hit your car. Other people saw me. They probably think that I'm leaving you my phone number, as I'm being very careful to write this and place it under your wiper. My very best to you for a wonderful life!"

It might be human to take the easy way out, rather than responsibly doing what we know we should. We have these moments of choice on many levels in our daily lives.

What Is Self-Control?

Self-control is subordinating our desires and impulses to our values. Many times the emotions of our "I Feel" overpower the logic of our "I Think." Our emotions and appetites win out over our logical thinking, causing us to suffer from low emotional control.

I had an old friend, now deceased, who was a gifted salesman and speaker. He was a jolly, wonderful, loving human being, but he couldn't control his appetites. He ate too much, drank too much, smoked, and spent too much. He dealt with it by constantly apologizing for his excesses. His self-esteem had eroded to the point of being tissue-thin.

Somewhere along the way his "wanting to do" began to take control over his "knowing what to do." A self-defeating cycle began. His actions triggered guilt. His guilt eroded his self-esteem. This caused his discipline to decay even more. His unconscious punishment strengthened the very behavior he knew he shouldn't do. His inability to control his appetites kept him on a success level that was far below his actual talents.

He made choices in his "I Think" that were in conflict with the inner wisdom of his "I Am." This conflict then triggered emotions of frustration, self-directed anger, and personal disgust.

At some point in our life, we must take control of our appetites and emotions. We must have the discipline to say "no." We need to subordinate our impulses to our values, and choose actions and responses that are congruent with them. We need to make choices that are consistent with our values, rather than standing by and allowing our "I Feel" to have unbridled rule of our choices and actions.

Maturity is a stuffy word. I must confess that even at my age, I haven't mastered this maturity thing. It seems that just as I can see growth in one or two areas, I discover that I have fallen back in others. I long ago came to grips with the belief that maturity is a progression and not necessarily a destination.

Are Our Decisions Congruent With Our Values?

For six months in 1980, I had the pleasure to work with W. Clement Stone. Reading his and Napoleon Hill's book, *Success Through a Positive Mental Attitude,* had helped turn my life around some years earlier. I learned from him and from his writings that he was a highly values-driven person. He adopted principles that guided his decisions, actions, and behaviors.

He had values-driven self-talk such as:

Have the courage to face the truth!

The truth will always be the truth!

When you have everything to gain and nothing to lose by trying, by all means try!

Even adversity brings with it the seeds of equivalent or greater benefit!

Do it now. Action is the thing!

Do the right thing because it's the right thing to do!

Through the process of self-suggestion he'd programmed these statements into his "I Am" so deeply that they became guiding values. Many times when he, or his people, had decisions to make, after analyzing possible solutions and actions he'd say, "We will do the right thing because it's the right thing to do!" He would then ask, "What is the right thing to do?" Usually the answer was quite evident, and action was taken in an attempt to do it.

I've noticed that highly successful people whose success endures have committed to strong, positive core values as their guidelines of behavior. These values then motivate their choices and decisions, and create an inner congruence that then triggers positive emotions of confidence, freedom, zest, and enthusiasm.

I see this lived out in my good friend Barry Griswell, CEO, president, and chairman of the Principal Financial Group, an international financial services organization. A man of impeccable integrity, he has done a terrific job in instilling strong values in his organization. Over and over I see how his values have been integrated into his company's culture, causing tremendous growth and profitability.

Each day we make values-based decisions. What we will do and what we won't do. Here are a few:

I eat to live rather than live to eat.

I give more than others expect, knowing this will open the floodgates for me to receive more than I expect.

I prosper to the extent that I fill the needs of my external and internal customers.

I do the right thing because it's the right thing to do.

I will strive to tell the truth, knowing that it will always set me free.

I look for the best in people, knowing that most will reciprocate and then look for the best in me.

I make every hour do the work of two.

I honor, praise, and thank my Creator daily.

I value people over things; relationships over possessions; and spiritual discernment over worldly wisdom.

All of us have values: core beliefs that guide our choices, decisions, and behavior. We each have a choice as to what values we have, and how they motivate our decisions. Our choices, then, have predictable consequences. Wisdom is selecting appropriate values that lead into high success.

It helps to know how to form the right values.

I'll challenge you to think about yours. I don't have the right, though, to tell you what they should be.

How Values Develop

Everyone has values. Some people's values are weaker, others stronger. Some people value honesty, truthfulness, and integrity; others value dishonesty, conning people, and taking advantage of them.

Values are developed several ways. Here are a few:

- Love that we either did or didn't experience in our formative years
- Our parents' beliefs and values
- Our parents' actions with each other and other people
- What we were taught as children
- What our peers value
- What seems to work in the lives of people we respect and admire
- What seems to be right when we take time to listen to our inner wisdom
- What happens when we seek guidance from the Divine Spirit within us

Then, whatever these values are, they powerfully influence our actions and behaviors.

Positive Versus Negative Values

Positive values attract, negative ones repel. I'll bet that you know this intuitively. You sense it when you're around people who exhibit strong, positive values such as enthusiasm, optimism, concern for others, non-judgmental acceptance of others, and healthy self-esteem.

You can take this concept of the power of thoughts, beliefs, and values and apply them in many directions and situations. Your own energy and strength. Your influence on others. Your influence on circumstances. And guess who gets to choose the kind of thoughts, beliefs, and values you have?

Yes, you guessed it, you!

Finding Your Core Values

Positive values are a necessary foundation for lasting success. The foundation must be carefully laid before the building, increased success, will stand solid. This brings us to the final and most important part of this chapter—deciding what you stand for.

I'm going to list several questions or categories and ask you to carefully respond to each. Get a pad of paper, or work on your computer, and respond to my questions in writing.

Please don't attempt to do this mentally, since it would have little or no value or payoff.

1. *How do I want customers and others to describe me?*
2. *How do I want to view myself?*
3. *What predominant frame of mind do I want to have?*
4. *How do I want to use my time?*
5. *How do I want to handle my money?*
6. *How do I want others to describe my behavior and attitudes at work?*
7. *What are my priorities in life?*
8. *How do I want customers and others to describe the way I listen to them?*
9. *How will I react to the negative responses, or offenses, of others?*
10. *How will I react to sudden life reversals?*
11. *How will I react to sudden life windfalls?*
12. *How will I react to praise of others?*
13. *How will I react to criticism from others?*
14. *What are my most prized possessions?*
15. *How do I deal with guilt?*
16. *How do I deal with people who have offended me?*
17. *How do I deal with people whom I have offended?*
18. *In what situations will I not tell the complete truth?*
19. *How will I decide between telling the truth and hurting another person?*
20. *To what extent am I an extra-mile person?*
21. *To what extent do I have a servant's heart?*
22. *How is integrity lived out in my life?*
23. *Do I see the glass half full or half empty?*

24. *Do I see problems as roadblocks or opportunities?*
25. *What do I think is the overall purpose of my life?*

Now that you've written some responses to the previous questions, please go back and prioritize them. Select the one that is the most important then, the next most important, and so on, until you've selected six. You may even want to get help from your spouse, a friend, or a co-worker. Both of you can work through these together.

Now, here's the most important part. Get a card and write your responses to the six areas you prioritized. These will become your core values. Your guiding principles. The boundaries of your behaviors. The filters through which you sift your future decisions, actions, and responses.

But before you write out your values, write at the top of your card your answer to the twenty-fifth question: *What do I think is the overall purpose of my life?* This will get you rethinking and examining your major purpose.

Don't get hung up thinking that selecting six of these is a life- or-death deal. Remember, you can change all these tomorrow, or anytime you want to do so. For now, just get started.

HOW TO GAIN THE MOST FROM THIS CHAPTER

You sell consistent *with* who you *are,* not *what* you *know.* Your values drive your sales behavior. Values are lighthouses that guide us through the storms and dark times of life. They define our boundaries. They become lines in the sand of our lives, across which we will not step. They carve out a distinct definition about who we are and who we're not.

You can best benefit from this chapter by doing the following activities:

1. Read this chapter through, underlining important points.
2. Write your purpose and core values on an index card, on your computer, and refer to it each day.
3. Observe others around you as you go about your day's activities, and identify their values.

4. Try to discover how others' values contribute to their success or lack of it.

Then, as you weave these through your selling activities, you'll program your core values into your unconscious "I Am" dimension.

Nothing will serve your long-term interests more than your espousal and demonstration of integrity and strong, sincere values.

Your success will increase when you can unconsciously say, "Who I am influences my long term sales success more than anything else."

13 DECIDING WHAT YOU STAND FOR

Assessment

Please take a few moments and check off the number that best describes your true, present beliefs, boundaries, or behaviors. Use these descriptors as guidelines.

5–Always true, without exception
4–Mostly true
3–True more often than not
2–True only part of the time
1–True only occasionally

1. I tell customers what I think they want to hear.	5 4 3 2 1 1 2 3 4 5	1. I tell the truth in all situations, unless it would be destructive to someone.
2. I never really think of values when setting goals.	5 4 3 2 1 1 2 3 4 5	2. My values influence the goals I set.
3. I need to make quick sales because of financial pressures.	5 4 3 2 1 1 2 3 4 5	3. I work on developing long-term relationships with clients.
4. I tend to put my selling face on when calling on customers.	5 4 3 2 1 1 2 3 4 5	4. I am the same person when selling as I am in a regular life situation.

5. I find it easy to change jobs when things get tough.	5 4 3 2 1	1 2 3 4 5	5. I steadfastly work through problems and difficulties.
6. My past actions reveal that I'll jump to greener pastures when things get tough.	5 4 3 2 1	1 2 3 4 5	6. My past actions prove that I'll hang tough in the face of adversity.
7. I frequently give in to my various appetites.	5 4 3 2 1	1 2 3 4 5	7. I'm well disciplined in all my appetites.
8. I value things over people.	5 4 3 2 1	1 2 3 4 5	8. I value people over things.
9. I do not have mentors who model strong values.	5 4 3 2 1	1 2 3 4 5	9. I have mentors who model strong values.
10. I'm mainly conscious of how my actions influence my success.	5 4 3 2 1	1 2 3 4 5	10. I'm conscious of how my inner beliefs influence my success.

- Add up the numbers in the right-hand column. _____
- Add up the numbers in the left-hand column. _____
- Subtract the left-hand column total from the right-hand column total and score yourself. _____

Assessments scoring guide is on page 35.

Keeping Score—Chapter 13

Behavior that gets evaluated, gets improved.

On a scale of 1–10, please evaluate your performance of each of these parts of the Breakthrough Process.

	S	M	T	W	T	F	S
1. I spent time thinking about my life purpose and core values today.							
2. I reviewed my values when I made decisions or communicated to customers today.							
3. I carefully observed others around me and identified their values that were demonstrated by their words and actions.							
4. I looked to discover how others' values contribute to their success or lack of it.							
Total Each Day							

Afterword

The psyche as a reflection of the world and man is a
thing of such infinite complexity that it can be observed
and studied from a great many sides.

—CARL JUNG

I've written this book to help you look at yourself from as many sides as my current knowledge and experience equip me to do. I sincerely hope that this journey into your "I Am" has opened up more questions than you now have answers for—that this state causes your quest for greater self-knowledge to be heightened.

Learning to sell well isn't really about learning how to sell well. As we have seen, it goes much deeper than that, into *who* you are—your values, self-beliefs, and purpose.

If I've helped you understand just a bit more about your true gifts and how to use them in serving people, I'll be well satisfied with my efforts—until I can learn, experience, and become more capable of taking you even deeper into the miracle within you.

Permit me to remind you that my purpose for this book has been to give you insights into what I believe professional selling success is. But even more important, it is to give you Action Guides to practice. It is the application of success principles, not the knowledge of them, that increases your success.

You probably didn't implement all the exercises I outlined for you. Now that you've completed the book, you may wish to go back from time to time and pick out chapters or exercises that speak to your needs. Look at it as an ongoing success guide that can help you through many levels of growth.

Jung wrote, "The finite will never be able to grasp the infinite." You and I will never totally fathom the potential power that inhabits our "I Am." But continuing the quest for greater understanding and effectiveness gives meaning to our lives.

May your quest enrich every part of your life.

About the Author

Ron Willingham is founder and CEO of Integrity Systems, Inc., an international training and development company with more than 1.5 million graduates in eighty nations. His organization is the leader in helping other organizations succeed with ethical, values-driven people development strategies. Integrity Systems's client list reads like a Who's Who in business: Johnson & Johnson, American Red Cross, IBM, The Guardian Life Insurance Co., Library of Congress, Franklin Templeton, Principal Financial Group, and more than two thousand others. He is the author of *Integrity Service,* as well as nine other books. More than twenty-six thousand facilitators have been certified to conduct his courses.